# INTRODUCTION

The aim of this book is to provide a comprehensive coverage in note form of
the GCE Ordinary level syllabuses in Psychology. Two separate syllabuses are
presently offered: the JMB Alternative/Ordinary level, and the AEB Or-
dinary/Alternative level in Psychology: Child Development. This book covers
the contents of both syllabuses, as follows.

The **JMB A/O Psychology syllabus** is dealt with in:

Chapter 1

Chapter 2:    sections on Early Experience; Socialisation; Development of Aggression; Sex Roles and Development of Self
Concept.

Chapter 4

Chapter 5:    sections on Behaviour Modification, Biofeedback and
Ageing and Senescence

The **AEB O/A Psychology: Child Development** syllabus is dealt with in:

Chapter 1:    sections on Learning and Conditioning and Maturation

Chapter 2

Chapter 3

Chapter 5:    sections on Behaviour Modification; Family, Home and
Surrogates; Play and Learning

Chapter 6

It should be stressed, nevertheless, that there is great value in encouraging
students to read beyond the boundaries set by the individual course studied
and the authors believe much will be gained by reading the whole of the text,
and not dealing merely with the sections particularly applicable to the set
syllabus.

*Pete Sanders*
*Liz Shaw*

365

by
# Pete Sanders, B.Sc., Dip. Couns.

Lecturer in Psychology
Wigan College of Technology

## and

# Liz Shaw, B.Sc., M.A.(Ed)

Lecturer in Psychology
Wigan College of Technology

# Casdec Ltd

729438

First Published 1982 by Casdec Ltd.
11 Windermere Avenue, Chester-le-Street,
Co. Durham.
© Casdec Ltd 1982

Reprinted 1983

Printed by The City Printing Works (Chester-le-Street) Ltd.,
Broadwood View, Chester-le-Street, Co. Durham, England DH3 3NJ

# CONTENTS

# 1

# BIOLOGICAL BASES OF BEHAVIOUR

## METHODS USED IN PHYSIOLOGICAL PSYCHOLOGY

Western scientific investigation tries to reduce the level of explanation of events, e.g. colour changes in photographic processes can be explained at the level of chemical reactions. Chemical reactions can themselves be explained in terms of the bonding properties of elements while bonding of elements can be explained in terms of their atomic structure. This approach is called **reductionism.** Reductionism is also evident as an approach to the explanation of psychological events, particularly in the area of physiological psychology, where an explanation of behaviour is sought in terms of biological structure and chemical reactions.

Information is collected from studies using a wide variety of methods, though it is possible to distinguish two broad approaches: firstly, interfering with the brain or nervous system and observing the effects on behaviour; secondly, interfering with behaviour or sensory stimulation and measuring the effects on the physiology of the subject.

1. **Methods of interfering with the brain**

(a) **Accidental injury:** Changes in behaviour as a result of accidents, tumours, strokes (and even slips of the surgeon's knife) have been a rich source of information and have resulted in some inspired deduction regarding brain function. E.g. P. Broca's work on the language areas of the brain (see p. 7).

(b) **Ablation:** The removal of brain tissue by surgical removal with a knife or suction, e.g. K. Lashley's work on learning and cortical function (see p.6).

(c) **Lesion:** The damage (rather than removal) of brain or nervous system tissue by various means: — cutting with a knife, burning with electrical current delivered through micro-electrodes or implantation of disabling chemicals.

(d) **Stimulation:** The brain or nervous system can be artificially excited in a highly controllable way using minute electrical currents passed through micro-electrodes or chemicals passed through micro-pipettes (very narrow tubes). Eg. Miller and DiCara's work (see p. 86).

2. **Methods of measuring physiological changes**

(a) **Electro-encephalogram (EEG):** This measures the electrical activity of the brain at the surface of the scalp (very occasionally on the surface of the cortex). Only large scale changes can be measured using this technique.

(b) **Micro-electrode recording:** Very small electrodes can be used to measure the electrical activity of small areas of the nervous system, often deep in the brain. Recordings can also be taken from single cells. Eg. the work of Hubel and Wiesel (see p. 31).

(c) **Galvanic Skin Response (GSR), Heart-rate, etc.:** A wide variety of physiological measures are taken as an indication of the arousal level or stress level of the subject. GSR is a measure of the electrical resistance of the skin and is a good indication of arousal.

(d) **Radioactive labelling:** When a radioactively labelled substance is injected into the bloodstream or is breathed in, it is possible to trace the path it takes in the blood vessels of the brain. Much has been learned of cortical function using this technique.

## STRUCTURE AND FUNCTION OF THE NERVOUS SYSTEM

1. **Nerve Cells**

Cells are the fundamental units of living organisms. During development of the foetus in the womb, the cells in each organ system in the body become increasingly specialised until each cell can only do one or two things really well.

The Nervous System is composed of nerve cells or **neurons** which occur in bundles called nerves, eg. optic nerve.

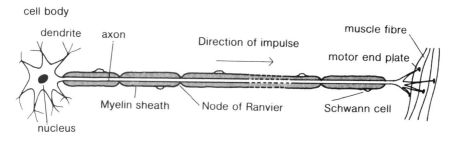

**Fig. 1.1 Typical Motor Neuron**

The neuron carries information in the form of electrochemical impulses in the long fibre or **axon** which extends from the cell body.

2

There are three main types of neuron:

(a)    Sensory neurons — carry impulses from the sense organs to the central nervous system (CNS).

(b)    Motor neurons — carry impulses from the CNS to the muscles causing muscle contraction.

(c)    Interconnecting neurons — found in the CNS, they link up to (i) connect sensory and motor neurons to form reflex arcs, and (ii) form more complicated chains of neurons connecting different parts of the CNS.

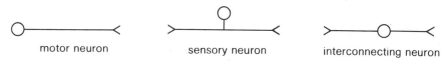

motor neuron        sensory neuron        interconnecting neuron

**Fig. 1.2 Diagrammatic representations of neurons**

Most neurons in the peripheral nervous system are covered with a fatty substance called **myelin** which is maintained by **schwann cells.** It is thought to insulate the neuron.

2.    **Impulses**

It is incorrect to think of a nerve impulse as electricity 'flowing' in a neuron. In its resting state the inside of the axon has fewer positively charged chemicals than the outside. An impulse is the momentary (between one and two milliseconds) reversal of this situation.

An impulse is generated by stimulation at one end of the neuron, either from a receptor which transduces physical energy, or from synaptic connections. The stimulus must be intense enough to take the neuron over it's **threshold potential.** If this happens an impulse is transmitted the entire length of the axon at full strength. If the threshold is not reached, no impulse is passes. Impulses do not vary in strength, they travel at full strength or not at all. This is known as the **all-or-none rule.**

This means that all nerve impulses are the same strength and duration. Information is carried in terms of the rate at which the neuron fires. Generally speaking, a strong stimulus produces a high firing rate whereas a weak stimulus produces a low firing rate. Some neurons send impulses in volleys in response to certain stimuli and other neurons may have a base firing rate (i.e. they continue to 'tick over' even when resting) in which case they can increase or decrease their firing rate when stimulated. This is called **coding** of information.

3.    **Synapses**

When neurons link up they do not make physical contact or touch each other. There is a small gap known as the **synapse** between adjoining neurons.

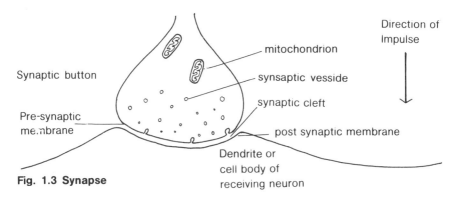

**Fig. 1.3 Synapse**

mitochondrion

Synaptic button

synsaptic vesside

synaptic cleft

Pre-synaptic me.nbrane

post synaptic membrane

Dendrite or cell body of receiving neuron

Direction of Impulse

When an impulse arrives at the synaptic button, the synaptic vessicles which have migrated towards the pre-synaptic membrane, burst and release their contents into the synaptic cleft. The substance released is called **transmitter substance,** and upon reaching the post-synaptic membrane causes the receiving neuron to fire (see excitatory and inhibitory synapses).

This break in the transmission of an impulse allows further coding to take place as follows:

Each neuron makes many synaptic connections with other neurons and in turn is stimulated by many other neurons.

**Summation:** if enough synapses are active, their combined effect may **add up** to exceed the threshold potential of the receiving neuron and cause it to fire.

**Excitatory synapses:** action of these synapses causes the receiving neuron to fire.

**Inhibitory synapses:** action of these synapses prevents the receiving neuron firing.

These features increase the flexibility of the nervous system in coding and transmitting information.

4. **The Nervous System**

The nervous system can be subdivided as follows:

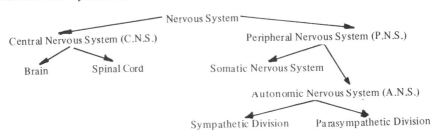

Nervous System

Central Nervous System (C.N.S.)

Peripheral Nervous System (P.N.S.)

Brain     Spinal Cord

Somatic Nervous System

Autonomic Nervous System (A.N.S.)

Sympathetic Division     Parasympathetic Division

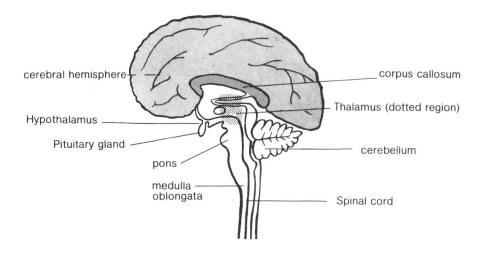

**Fig. 1.4 Central Nervous System**

**Spinal Cord:** composed of grey matter (cell bodies and non-myelinated fibres) and white matter (myelinated fibres). Its main function is to conduct impulses to and from the brain (it connects the CNS and PNS) but it also controls a number of fairly complex reflex actions, some with no brain involvement at all.

**Brain Stem:** contains autonomic nervous system nucleii which control breathing, heartbeat, blood pressure etc. Also contains the Reticular Formation or Reticular Activating System (RAS) which is concerned with sleep, arousal and attention and also provides an indirect route to the cortex for sensory information.

**Cerebellum:** its principal role is the control of fine muscle movements. All motor information passes through it and it also receives information from the balance sensors in the inner ear.

**Hypothalamus:** consists of more than 20 nucleii — anterior and medial nucleii relate to parasympathetic function, posterior nucleii relate to sympathetic functions (see below). Its special role is the co-ordination and integration of responses into patterns of activity e.g. eating, drinking, sexual behaviour etc. Many of these activity patterns are concerned with maintenance of the internal environment or **homeostasis.**

**Thalamus:** consists of many inter-connected nucleii — some connect sub-cortical structures only, some relay sensory information to the cortex. Each sense has its own respective nucleii, the direct route (as opposed to the indirect route — see brainstem). Other routes relay motor information from the cortex to the cerebellum. It has the appropriate title 'relay station of the brain'.

**Cerebral Hemisphere:** the wrinkled surface of these hemispheres consists of cell bodies only — grey matter — and is called the **cerebral cortex.**

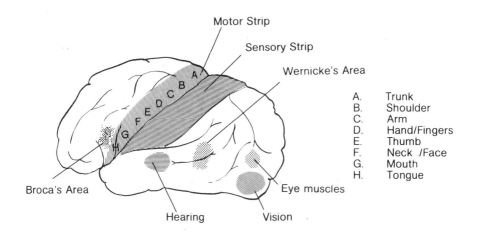

Fig. 1.5 **The Surface of the left cerebral hemisphere**

The region enveloped by the cortex consists mainly of fibres connecting the various cortical regions. The motor and sensory areas are connected to the brainstem and ultimately spinal cord via the thalamus and are subject to varying degrees of crossover of fibres. (Except the nerves serving the eye, ear, nose and face. These are **cranial nerves** and enter and exit the brain directly).

5.   **Localisation of Functions on the Cortex**
(a)   In the 1920's K. Lashley conducted many experiments on the effects of lesioning and ablation of cortical tissue in rats in order to discover the area(s) responsible for learning and memory. He was unsuccessful — such areas could not be found. The memories of the rats seemed to be equally spread out over the whole cortex and how much the rats 'forgot' depended on the *amount* of cortical tissue removed or destroyed, not *where* it was. He called this the 'Law of mass action.'
(b)   The motor and sensory 'strips' of the cortex were mapped in some detail in the 1950's by brain surgeons such as W. Penfield. Using various methods of stimulation at the surface of the cortex (including touch and electricity) the sensations and bodily responses of several patients

undergoing brain surgery were recorded. Although the majority of the patients were epileptic, the results have been borne out in subsequent studies of accident and stroke victims.

(c) The careful observation and post-mortem examination of brain damaged patients in the nineteenth century by P. Broca and C. Wernicke led to the identification of two language areas on the left hemisphere. Wernicke's area is responsible for the understanding of spoken language, and Broca's area responsible for the production of speech.

(d) The two hemispheres of the cerebrum seem to have different functions. By cutting the corpus callosum a so called 'split-brain' is created. Such work suggests that left hemisphere controls language functions, and the right hemisphere oversees visuo-spatial functions.

(e) Recent evidence from the recovery of stroke patients using physiotherapy and the use of radioactively labelled chemicals with adults who successfully overcame hydrocephaly as children, suggests that the localisation of cortical function is nowhere near as rigid as was first thought.

## 6. The Peripheral Nervous System: The Somatic Nervous System

The somatic nervous system is concerned with all the voluntary movements made by the body and all the sensory information from the receptors in the eyes, ears, nose, tongue, muscles and skin. The cell bodies of the motor neurons are inside the CNS; the myelinated axons travelling to the muscles outside the CNS, whereas all but a millimetre or so of the sensory neurons lie outside the CNS.

## 7. The Peripheral Nervous System: The Autonomic Nervous System

The autonomic nervous system regulates the activity of the internal organs — heart, blood vessels, intestines etc. thereby co-ordinating the largely *involuntary* activities of heart rate, blood pressure, digestion etc.

The nerves supplying internal organs are non-myelinated and the cell bodies of the motor neurons are found in **ganglia** outside the CNS. The ANS is sub-divided into the sympathetic and parasympathetic divisions. Generally speaking the sympathetic division speeds bodily systems up and prepares the organism for activity, whereas the parasympathetic division slows the body down, conserving resources. Fibres from *both* divisions supply most organs and have an antagonistic effect, see table below.

| Organ or System | Effect of Sympathetic Action | Effect of Parasympathetic Action |
| --- | --- | --- |
| Heart | Heart beat speeded up | Heart beat slowed down |
| Blood vessels in skin, intestines, etc | Constriction (narrowing) | |
| Blood vessels in voluntary muscles | Dilation (widening) | |
| Liver | Sugar released | Sugar stored |
| Intestines | Peristalsis slowed or stopped | Peristalsis speeded up |
| Pupil of eye | Dilation | Contraction |

The autonomic nervous system operates in close co-ordination with the endocrine system. There are many points of close contact and liaison between the two systems:

1 . The effects of the Sympathetic division mirror the effects of the hormone adrenalin, primarily because the transmitter substance used at the nerve-muscle junction is nor-adrenalin, a substance nearly identical to adrenalin.

2 . The site of control of the ANS is the hypothalamus, which is immediately above the pituitary gland in the brain. The pituitary gland controls and co-ordinates the action of the endocrine system.

## EMOTION

### Involvement of the CNS and ANS in Emotion

The three best known explanations of the possible physiological and cognitive processes underpinning emotion are as follows:

(i) **William James and Carl Lange** independently advanced theories in the late 19th century but because of similarities their approach is often referred to as the James-Lange theory. They believed that emotion was experienced as a result of feedback from bodily changes that take place in response to a frightening or upsetting situation e.g. a sudden stumble on the stairs causes your heart to pound and your respiration rate to increase, which you recognise and interpret as the feeling of fear.

(ii) **Cannon** in the 1920's noticed that bodily changes do not seem to differ much from one emotional state to another. Associated with this are the facts that the internal organs are not richly supplied with sensory neurons so would not be able to provide much feedback, and artificial induction of the bodily changes associated with emotion does not produce 'true' feelings of emotion. Cannon suggested that the thalamus responded to an emotion producing stimulus by simultaneously sending impulses to both activate the ANS and inform the cortex leading to perception of the feeling of emotion.

We now know it is the hypothalamus, not the thalamus, which is instrumental in co-ordinating ANS responses, and that a powerful factor in feelings of emotion is the whole range of cognitive activities e.g. perception and appraisal of the external situation, memories and past experiences etc.

(iii) **Schacter and Singer (1959)** included such cognitive factors in a theory of emotion which was supported by the results of an involved experiment. They produced physiological arousal by injecting the subjects with adrenalin, telling them they had received a vitamin injection. Some subjects were correctly informed about the effects of the injection (pounding heart, trembling limbs etc.) some were misinformed (told to expect itching, numbness and headache) and some were given no information about possible side effects. A control group of subjects were given a saline injection and no information about side effects.

The subjects were then placed in the presence of a confederate of the experimenter who was scripted to act in either a euphoric, happy way or an angry, complaining way. Neither the control group nor the subjects that were correctly informed were affected by the mood of the confederate. The subjects who were misinformed and those given no information reported they felt happy if accompanied by the happy 'stooge,' and angry if accompanied by the angry 'stooge.' They were obviously basing their interpretation of their own bodily changes on the cognitive information provided by the external situation.

## SENSORY INFORMATION PROCESSING

1. **Visual System**

   The visual system comprises the eyes, optic nerves, visual pathways (including the superior colliculi and lateral geniculate nucleii) and the visual cortex of the brain.

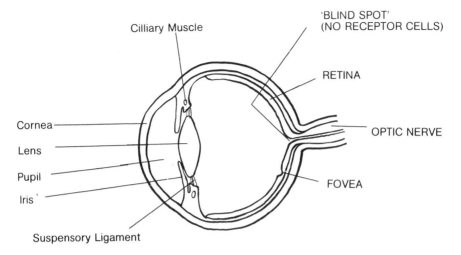

**Fig. 1.6 The Eye**

Light from external objects enters the eye and is refracted to form a rough image on the retina by the curved cornea. The lens completes the fine focussing and also has the ability to change shape under tension from the ciliary muscle. When the lens is stretched flat by relaxation of the ciliary muscle, it can focus on distant objects; when allowed to assume its naturally more spherical shape, it can focus on near objects. This process is called **accommodation,** its purpose is to form a sharp image on the retina where the light sensitive receptor cells transduce the light into nerve impulses.

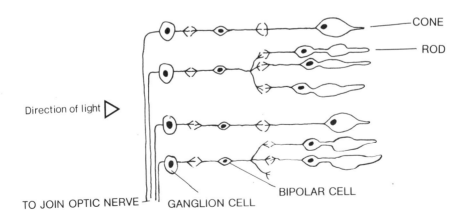

**Fig. 1.7 The Retina**

The retina contains two types of receptor cells:

**Rods** are used in conditions of low light intensity, and give a grainy image (because they are not packed very close together) in black and white (actually, dark purple because of the photopigment rhodopsin).

**Cones** are used in high light intensity conditions (daylight and normal electric light) and give a sharp detailed colour image. It is easy to determine whether any cones are working by simply looking for colours. If you can see in colour, there is enough light to stimulate your cones.

Both rods and to a lesser extent cones demonstrate sensory adaptation (as do most kinds of receptor). They can alter the amount of active pigment available at any one time so as to exploit the widest possible range of light conditions. This is best observed when moving from bright light to low light conditions: we say our eyes 'get used to' the dark.

Rods and cones are not evenly distributed around the retina. The area known as the **fovea** contains relatively few rods but is packed with cones. It is this region of the retina that receives the image at the centre of our gaze and gives us greatest visual acuity. Moving away from the fovea we find more rods and fewer cones per square millimetre and fewer receptors generally.

## 2. Colour Vision

The mechanism by which we see in colour is not fully understood. The simplest theory suggests there are three kinds of cone in the retina with their maximum sensitivity in the red, blue and green parts of the visible spectrum respectively. Thus, according to the relative numbers of each type of cell firing, the brain can deduce an impression of colour. Unfortunately, although there is evidence to suggest that their are three kinds of cones responding to different wavelengths of light, the colours concerned are not those expected.

The 'opponent-process' theory suggests there are three types of receptor, each producing two outputs; one during the breakdown of photopigments and one during their reconstitution. Each type of receptor would give information about a primary colour and its antagonist e.g. one would signal blue or yellow, another red or green and the third black or white. However, this is not supported by the latest physiological evidence.

## 3. Visual Pathways

The optic nerve exits the eye split down the middle, one half carrying information from the left hand side of the retina and the other half carrying information from the right hand side of the retina. At the optic chiasma the optic nerve divides and crosses over so that the right hand visual field is represented on the left hand side of the brain and vice-versa (see Fig.1.8).

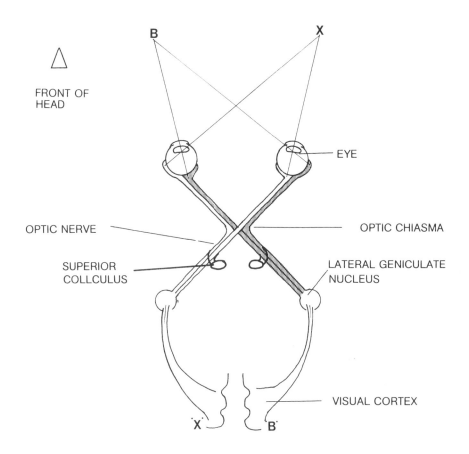

FRONT OF HEAD

B

X

EYE

OPTIC NERVE

OPTIC CHIASMA

SUPERIOR COLLCULUS

LATERAL GENICULATE NUCLEUS

VISUAL CORTEX

X'

B'

**FIG. 1.8 The Visual Pathways**

The function of the superior colliculus seems to be to locate objects in the visual field and possibly have some role in directing eye movements. The lateral geniculate nuclei are little understood and although well laid out with well ordered rows and columns of cells, the best that can be said is that, being thalamic nuclei, they act as relay stations.

The visual cortex also presents itself as a highly ordered area, but thanks to pioneering work by Hubel and Wiesel (1959-66) we know something of its function.

It is thought that there are at least three types of cortical cell involved; simple, complex and hypercomplex cortical cells process the incoming signals in turn and are sensitive to more and more detailed aspects of the stimuli.

## 4.   The Auditory System

Sound entering the outer ear sets the ear drum vibrating, which in turn sets the ossicles into motion. The final middle ear bone, the stapes, vibrates with a piston-like motion and causes the fluids in the inner ear to move. Because fluid cannot be compressed, the pressure is released by a distortion of the round window membrane in harmony with the stapes-induced distortion of the oval window (see Figs. 1.9 and 1.10).

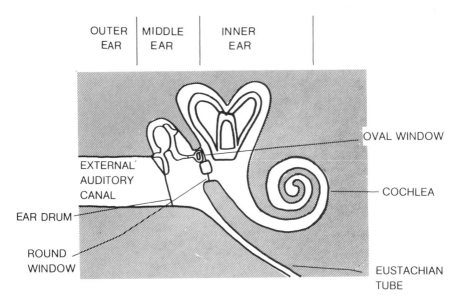

OUTER EAR | MIDDLE EAR | INNER EAR

OVAL WINDOW

EXTERNAL AUDITORY CANAL

COCHLEA

EAR DRUM

ROUND WINDOW

EUSTACHIAN TUBE

**Fig. 1.9 A section through the human ear**

It is in the cochlea that sound is transduced into nervous energy by the hair cells and their supporting tissues, collectively known as the **organ of corti.**

As the fluid pressure selectively distorts regions of the basilar membrane, so the hair cells at different points along the cochlea fire and send impulses down the auditory nerve.

## 5.   Perception of Loudness

As with coding of intensity generally, it is thought that loudness is coded by an increase in the firing rate of the hair cells, so the louder the sound, the higher the rate of firing.

## 6.   Perception of Pitch

The basilar membrane is reinforced with transverse fibres that resonate in response to different frequencies as a result of their differing lengths and tension. Experiments show that for low frequency sound (below 1000 Hz) the upper region of the basilar membrane vibrates as a whole sending volleys of impulses along the auditory nerve. Above 1000 Hz the region of resonance moves 'down' the cochlea with the highest frequencies causing the hair cells at the end nearest the middle ear to fire. This is known as 'place theory,' because the position of the firing hair cells along the cochlea signals the frequency of sound heard.

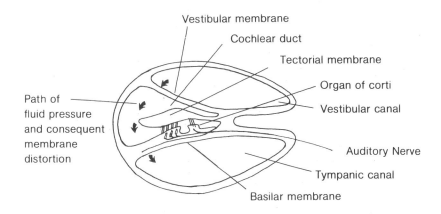

**Fig. 1.10 A section through the cochlea**

## THE BASIC MECHANISMS OF HEREDITY

1.    **Chromosomes and Genes**
    The nucleus of each living cell in the body contains **chromosomes**. Although invisible except during cell division, it is known that there is a fixed number for each species of plant or animal, e.g. fruit flies have 8, mice have 40 and human beings 46. This full complement for any species is known as the **diploid number**. Chromosomes exist in pairs, so each human cell nucleus contains 23 pairs.
    The chromosomes contain the information (in chemical form) which enables each cell to specialise during foetal development so that the new individual possesses all the particular characteristics of its species. This information is carried in small units or **genes,** each gene constitutes one small component of

14

the overall genetic instructions of **code** contained on each chromosome. So one gene may specify whether a person is to have blue eyes or brown, and another will determine whether they will have fair hair or dark.

## 2.  Cell Division and Gametes

Two types of cell division takes place within the human body. **Mitosis** is the kind that replenishes dead tissue e.g. under the skin or in the bone marrow to make new blood cells. **Meiosis** takes place in the testes and ovaries only and is the process whereby sex cells (sperms and eggs) or **gametes** are formed. During meiosis the number of chromosomes present in the nucleus is halved. This is known as the **haploid number.** So each gamete has only 23 chromosomes **not** arranged in pairs, (since these have broken up during meiosis) half the diploid number.

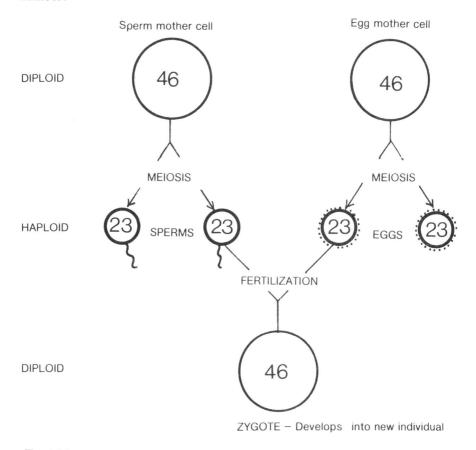

**Fig. 1.11**

15

Thus each child receives half its chromosomes from each parent.

The sex of each individual is determined by the so-called **sex chromosomes,** denoted 'X' and 'Y'. In females these two chromosomes are both X chromosomes, while in the male, one is an X chromosome and one is a Y chromosome. During meiosis this pair of sex chromosomes is separated in the same way as others so that all eggs contain X chromosomes, but half of the sperms will contain Y chromosomes.

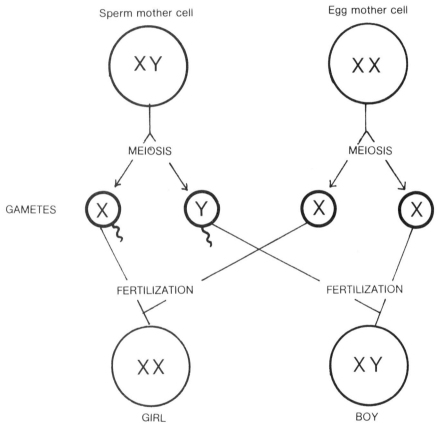

**Fig. 1.12**

## 3. Twins

Twins may be either **monozygotic** (identical) the result of separation of a single fertilized egg into two distinct embryos, or **dizygotic** (fraternal) the result of simultaneous fertilization of two separate eggs by two separate sperms. Identical twins therefore have identical sets of chromosomes since they are formed by mitosis from a single zygote. Fraternal twins have sets of chromosomes that are very different, and will be no more alike than any normal borthers or sisters.

### 4.   Nature — Nurture Debate

One source of data in the nature — nurture debate is identical twins since it can be argued that differences between them are due to the effects of the environment (because they have identical genetic codes). Many studies compare identical twins reared apart, identical twins reared together, non-identical twins reared together and siblings. It is well known that identical twins closely resemble each other and are always the same sex, yet it is still difficult to separate the effects of heredity from those of child-rearing practices.

## MATURATION

Since the genetic code controls the specialisation of cells in foetal development, it has been suggested that this influence may extend beyond birth. This apparently pre-programmed physical and physiological development after birth is called **maturation.** It is of obvious relevance to psychologists since changes in structure may influence the development of behaviour, e.g. the onset of sexual maturity in many species heralds courtship and sexual behaviour. Also if physical structure develops via maturation, perhaps certain behaviours are also maturationally determined.

**Dennis (1940).** Children of the Hopi indians (a tribe of North American indians) are traditionally kept bound to a cradle board for the first six months of life. They have little or no opportunity to crawl or practice walking movements. Dennis found that such children walk at the same age as other children in the tribe whose parents did not practice the traditional binding. This suggests that maturation, not practice is the main factor in the acquisition of walking.

However, this was not a properly controlled experiment, as the families were not allocated to the conditions at random, so any number of variables might have contributed to the result.

**Gesell and Thompson (1929).** A pair of orphaned identical twins were raised in near-identical conditions in a nursing home. At 46 weeks of age one twin was given motor skill training e.g. stair-climbing for 20 minutes per day for six weeks. When tested at 53 weeks the trained twin climbed the stairs in 17 seconds and the untrained twin climbed the stairs in 40 seconds. After three weeks training the untrained twin was as competent as her sister. Gesell believed that the results showed the effect of maturation in locomotor skills. However, both twins were allowed to crawl freely during the experimental period and the practice consisted of lifting the twin from stair to stair.

17

**Cruze (1935).** In an ingenious study using newly hatched chicks, Cruze demonstrated the interaction of maturation and practice in the development of pecking accuracy. Using five groups of hand-fed dark-reared chicks, he tested their pecking accuracy at 24, 48, 72, 96 and 120 hours old respectively, noting their improvement. He then allowed each group 12 hours practice and found that there was a steady improvement with age (maturation) yet at any age, the 12 hours practice greatly improved performance.


## LEARNING AND CONDITIONING

The term **'learning'** covers a very wide range of procedures and phenomena in a range of situations, described by many different types of psychologist. Kimble defined learning as 'a relatively permanent change in behaviour as a result of practice.' **'Conditioning'** on the other hand is a more specific term used to describe the acquisition of a new pattern of behaviour under certain conditions.

There are two basic procedures whereby a new pattern of behaviour can be acquired: **classical conditioning** and **instrumental conditioning.** Whether these two procedures result in different types of behaviour acquisition is a question still debated by psychologists, so it is safer to limit our discussion at 'O' level to the procedures only.

### 1.   Classical Conditioning

As knowledge of the structure and function of the N.S. increased, many physiologists turned to the reflex arc (the most basic working combination of neurones in any N.S.) to help explain behaviour. I.P. Pavlov (1849-1936) a Russian physiologist engaged in the study of the salivary reflex, stumbled upon the procedure which we now call classical conditioning. Pavlov's basic experiment involved a dog which had previously undergone simple surgery to expose the salivary duct to enable Pavlov to measure the response in terms of the number of drops of saliva secreted. The basic experiment followed these steps:

| Procedure | Result |
|---|---|
| 1. Sound tuning fork (C.S.) alone to ⟶ ensure it doesn't cause salivation *before* conditioning. (This is a **control**). | Orientation responses. (Ears pricking, head turning, etc.) |
| 2. Puff meat powder (U.C.S.) into dogs ⟶ mouth to measure salivation reflex. | Salivation. (U.C.R.) |

3. Present sound of tuning fork (C.S.) at ——➤ Salivation. (U.C.R.)
   the same time as blowing meat powder
   (U.C.S.) into dog's mouth. (Called
   **pairing**).

4. Repeat pairing several times.————————➤ Salivation. (U.C.R.)

5. Present the sound of the tuning fork ——➤ Salivation. (C.R.)
   (C.S.) alone (Test trial).

C.S. : Conditional Stimulus — Sound of tuning fork.
C.R. : Conditional Response — Salivation to sound of tuning fork.
U.C.S. : Unconditional Stumulus — Meat powder.
U.C.R. : Unconditional Response — Salivation to meat powder.

Pavlov described the relationship between the meat powder and the salivation to it as **unconditional.** In other words it does not depend on anything else, but happens automatically, and is a reflex. The procedure of conditioning transfers the salivation response from the natural stimulus of meat powder in the mouth, to the unnatural stimulus of the sound of a tuning fork. This relationship he called **conditional,** i.e. it depends upon the conditioning procedure, and does not happen naturally.

The process by which it is thought the new behaviour pattern is acquired is called **contiguous association,** i.e. when two events occur close together in time and space we often think that they are linked (associated) e.g. a child links the click of the light switch with the illumination of the bulb long before it is old enough to understand the principles of electricity. The nervous system of the dog links the sound of the tuning fork with the existing salivary reflex.

## 2. Generalisation
This is the phenomenon of conditional responses being made to stimuli which are similar to the original conditional stimulus. Also, the more similar the stimulus is to the original C.S., the stronger the C.R. e.g. if, in his experiment, Pavlov had used a tuning fork that vibrated at 500Hz, then the dog might respond to similar tones as follows:

19

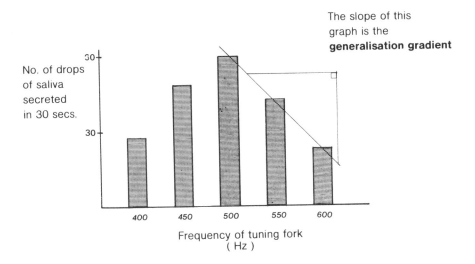

Fig. 1.13

Exactly what constitutes a 'similar' stimulus is debatable, certainly it is difficult to predict which stimuli might cause a response in any given situation. Animals seem able to detect similarities between stimuli which often do not occur to the human experimenters.

### 3. Discrimination

Consider the following procedure:

1. Tuning fork A(500 Hz) paired with meat powder.————➤ Salivation
2. Tuning fork B(550 Hz) paired with **no** meat powder.——➤ Salivation
(Generalisation)

On repeated presentation of these two pairings the salivation to tuning fork B(550 Hz) lessens and dies away after a few trials. The animal can discriminate or *tell the difference between* the two stimuli.

If the animal is presented with two stimuli so similar that it can't tell the difference between them, it becomes extremely disturbed and responds at random. Pavlov did this with dogs by expecting them to discriminate between a circle and a series of ever more circular eclipses. He called the subsequent breakdown in the dog's behaviour **Experimental Neurosis.** Although there are many differences between these experiments and the rich complexity of human disturbance, many psychologists seek understanding of human neurosis in terms of the basic principles of conditioning.

## 4.  Extinction

If a new behaviour pattern is acquired in this way, after a number of presentations of the C.S. alone the C.R. will die away and eventually cease. This is called extinction.

This process does not return the animal to its original state prior to conditioning. If we interrupt the continued lone presentation of the C.S. with a loud noise, the C.R. returns (albeit in a slightly weaker form). This is called **disinhibition,** because Pavlov believed that extinction was an inhibiting force opposite to conditioning and that the loud noise briefly removed the inhibition.

A similar result is achieved when a rest period is inserted after extinction. The C.R. returns again. This is called **spontaneous recovery.** Eventually after many interruptions or rest periods, and ever more weak recoveries, the C.R. disappears altogether. But even then an animal so treated will relearn the response faster than a naive animal.

## 5.  Higher Order Conditioning

This involves using the C.S. from one situation as the U.C.S. in another, e.g. the tuning fork in Pavlov's experiment. After getting it to consistently elicit salivation, it could be paired with another stimulus, say a light, as follows:

1.  Tuning fork (C.S.) + meat powder (U.C.S.) ⟶ Salivation (U.C.R.)
2.  Tuning fork (C.S.) ⟶ Salivation (C.R.)
3.  Light (C.S.) + tuning fork (U.C.S.¹) ⟶ Salivation (U.C.R.¹)
4.  Light (C.S.) ⟶ Salivation (C.R.)

This procedure can sometimes be repeated several times before the C.R. weakens too much, though it is more successfully achieved with a noxious U.C.S. such as electric shock and paw withdrawal as the U.C.R.

## 6.  Instrumental Conditioning

Just after the turn of the century, at the same time that Pavlov was carrying out his experiments on classical conditioning, an American psychologist, E.L. Thorndike (1874-1949) described the principle which formed the basis for what we now call instrumental conditioning. He called this principle the **Law of Effect** and slightly reworded it reads: 'a piece of behaviour stands a greater chance of being repeated under similar circumstances if it is followed by a reward.' He extracted this principle from his work with cats in puzzle boxes. He would place a hungry cat in a box from which it could see food. In order to escape and reach the food, the cat had to operate some mechanism — pull string, a bolt or a lever.

By pacing the box and pawing at the bars, the cat would eventually accidentally operate the mechanism and escape. Each time the cat was replaced in the box it took successively less and less time to escape. For fairly obvious reasons Thorndike called this **Trial and Error Learning.**

Much research followed this using white rats running in mazes. Rats are more convenient than cats to house and handle, and mazes are better than puzzle boxes for manipulating variables. If we measure the time spent running such a maze or the number of errors (wrong turns) made over successive trials, and plot the results we see a typical **learning curve.**

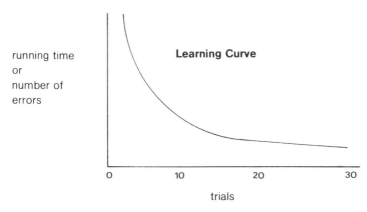

**Fig. 1.14**

In the 1930's B.F. Skinner extended the horizons of instrumental conditioning by inventing apparatus which made the measurement of behaviour both easier and more sensitive. He also tried to isolate and name the essential elements of instrumental conditioning (rather like Pavlov had done with classical conditioning) so that the principles could be generalised beyond the laboratory situation.

He called the behaviour which is rewarded the **operant.** He renamed instrumental conditioning, **operant conditioning.** He called the reward a **reinforcer** — so the event which immediately follows (and therefore increases the likelihood of) the operant is the reinforcer. To Skinner and his co-workers it seemed that operant conditioning could not take place without a reinforcer.

The apparatus devised by Skinner came to be called a **Skinner box,** and consisted of a small chamber in which the animal was presented with stimuli and reinforcements:

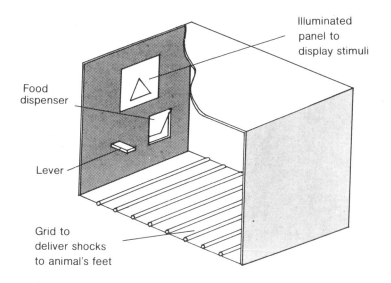

Illuminated panel to display stimuli

Food dispenser

Lever

Grid to deliver shocks to animal's feet

**Fig. 1.15 Skinner Box**

### 7.   Behaviour Shaping

When an animal is first placed in a Skinner box, it is nervous. It is necessary to train the animal to feed from the food dispenser and press the lever to obtain food and operate the apparatus which records the responses. The experimenter does this by reinforcing behaviour which successively approximates pressing the lever, e.g. the animal will spontaneously explore the chamber, sniffing and leaning on the walls. When it is facing the wall with the levers, the experimenter dispenses a food pellet, thus reinforcing the animal facing the wall. Then the animal may, in its continued exploration, sniff the lever. It is immediately reinforced for this and eventually the animal is brought towards the desired response — that of lever pressing. This is called **behaviour shaping.**

### 8.   Generalisation

This is a feature of instrumental conditioning also. The animal can offer a variety of similar but incomplete responses to lever pressing — e.g. biting the lever or only half pressing it. This is called **response generalisation.** Also, the animal will make some responses to situations which are similar but not identical to the one in which it was originally conditioned this is called **stimulus generalisation.** E.g. if a rat is reinforced when a 1 inch diameter circle is presented, it will also press the bar to similar sized circles.

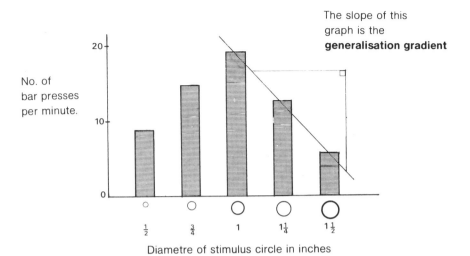

**Fig. 1.16**

### 9. Discrimination

This is similar to classical conditioning. Here the rat is reinforced only when it presses the bar in the presence of the 1 inch circle, but *not* when the 1¼ inch circle is present. After a few trials the bar pressing decreases and stops in the presence of the 1¼ inch circle. The animal has discriminated between the two stimuli.

### 10. Extinction

When reinforcement ceases, the operant response decreases and stops after a number of trials. Disinhibition and spontaneous recovery take place as in classical conditioning.

### 11. Reinforcement

There are two types of event which can follow an operant response, pleasant and unpleasant and the experimenter can either give them or take them away, so there are four ways of manipulating these events:

| | Stimulus given | Stimulus taken away |
|---|---|---|
| Pleasant stimulus (Food or escape) | Positive reinforcement | Omission |
| Unpleasant stimulus (Electric shock) | Punishment | Negative reinforcement |

It is obvious that punishment and negative reinforcement are not the same. Negative reinforcement is often called **escape learning** (not to be confused with the cat in the puzzle box). This has been thoroughly investigated using the **shuttle box,** in which an animal leaps to and fro across a central barrier to escape an electric shock to its feet. If the rat is given a warning (a buzzer sounding) it can learn to jump before the shock occurs. This is called **avoidance learning.** The components of escape and avoidance learning are very similar to classical conditioning.

One of Skinner's most notable contributions was the introduction of **reinforcement schedules.** When reinforcements are not given for every response it is called **partial reinforcement.** There are four basic variations of partial reinforcement schedules:

1.  **Fixed Ratio:** one reinforcement is given every so many lever presses, e.g. F.R.5 schedule gives one pellet of food every 5 responses. This yields a fast response rate.
2.  **Variable Ratio:** one pellet of food is given **on average** every, say, 5 lever presses. The actual reinforcement is not necessarily delivered on every 5th response.
3.  **Fixed Interval:** one pellet of food is given after each fixed interval of time, say 1 minute, but only if at least one response is made in the time interval.
4.  **Variable Interval:** one pellet of food is given **on average** every so many minutes, though the actual reinforcement does not necessarily arrive each minute. At least one response per interval must be made to obtain a reward.

The effect of partial reinforcement is considerable, both generally (it yields a faster response rate and greater resistance to extinction than continuous reinforcement) and specifically (each schedule has its own particular characteristics with regards to response rate and extinction).

| Schedule | Response rate | Extinction rate |
|---|---|---|
| Continuous (CRF) | Very slow | Very fast |
| Fixed Ratio (FR) | Fast | Medium |
| Fixed Interval (FI) | Medium | Medium |
| Variable Ratio (VR) | Fast | Slow |
| Variable Interval (VI) | Fast | Very Slow |

The events that we have looked at so far in the role of reinforcer are **primary reinforcers** those that have a direct effect upon the animal. If a neutral stimulus and primary reinforcer are paired, the neutral stimulus takes on the properties of the primary reinforcer and can itself be used as a reinforcer. The neutral stimulus has become a **secondary reinforcer,** e.g. the food dispensing mechanism in Skinner boxes always make a noise. This noise soon becomes associated with the food and the noise itself can then be used as a reinforcer, i.e. the animal will press the lever just to hear the noise in the absence of food. An example of a secondary reinforcer from human experience is money.

12. **Similarities and Differences Between Classical and Instrumental Conditioning**
There is continued debate whether there really are two different types of conditioning or whether both classical and instrumental are just different versions of the same basic process.

(a) **Similarities.** Both forms of conditioning have a phase of **acquisition** as a result of reinforced practice and demonstrate extinction as a result of non-reinforced practice. In both cases, extinction can be interrupted by spontaneous recovery. Although not unique to conditioning, both classical and instrumental conditioning demonstrate generalisation and discrimination.

Both forms of conditioning are achieved (it is widely thought) by virtue of the contiguous association of two events.

(b) **Differences**

| Classical conditioning | Instrumental conditioning |
|---|---|
| The response (salivation) depends upon the reinforcement (U.C.S. food). | Reinforcement (pellet of food) depends upon the response (lever press). |
| One reinforcer can elicit only one type of response e.g. food leads only to salivation. | One reinforcer can be used to strengthen a wide variety of responses. |
| Partial reinforcement weakens and disrupts conditioning if the C.S.-U.C.S. pairing is diluted more than 33%. | Partial reinforcement in the form of schedules greatly strengthens instrumental conditioning. |
| Only involuntary, reflexive behaviour can be classically conditioned. | Voluntary (and possibly involuntary behaviour via biofeedback — see page 86) can be instrumentally conditioned. |

## 13. Learning and Performance

Suppose we ask a subject (S) to learn a route on a map, and to test this learning we wait for S to arrive. If S arrives safely, we assume S has learned the route correctly (in fact S may have made a series of wild guesses). If S fails to arrive we assume S failed to learn the route. But there are alternative explanations — S may have correctly **learned** the route but a) sprained an ankle on the way or b) had been confused by a diversion due to road works. When we try to measure learning we always measure **performance** as well. It is not possible to measure learning directly.

This distinction was highlighted by E.C. Tolman who showed that rats who were given non-reinforced experience of a maze appeared to learn the maze. This learning did not become apparent until the rats were reinforced half-way through the experiment, suggesting that reinforcement is responsible for the performance of learning but not the learning itself. (See also Bandura, Ross and Ross page 59). This is called **Latent Learning**.

## 14. Transfer of Learning

When an animal learns a new pattern of behaviour it affects its subsequent learning of other new behaviours. It can be helpful in new learning situations or it can hinder learning in new situations. This is called **transfer of learning** and it can be positive (helpful) or negative (unhelpful). Thus, a tennis player might find previous experience helpful when learning to play squash but a hindrance when trying to learn badminton.

H. Harlow demonstrated a particular type of positive transfer when he presented monkeys with pairs of differently patterned objects. Under one of the objects was a raisin. The monkey was allowed to look under one object in each trial, so the optimum strategy would be to look under the remaining object in the second trial. The monkeys did no better than chance at first in their attempts to obtain the raisin. After 200 similar problems (with different patterns or objects) the monkeys chose the correct object about 90% of the time on the second trial. The monkeys seemed to have learned the *principle* involved in this type of problems. Harlow also used a three-item puzzle in which the monkey had to select the odd one out. Harlow found similar results after the monkeys had been exposed to around 200 or so problems of the same type but with different objects or patterns. The principles or rules which enable the monkeys to solve the problems are called a **Learning Set.** Learning sets have a distinct advantage over trial and error learning, which at best gives a learning rate equal to chance.

# 2
# COGNITIVE DEVELOPMENT

## METHODS IN DEVELOPMENTAL PSYCHOLOGY

Developmental psychology attempts to study people as they change over time. Most research in developmental psychology has been concerned with children and old age.

In order to attempt to understand development, different methods are used.

1.  **Experiments**
    (See page 102).
    **Disadvantages.** Children may be disturbed by the unnatural surroundings or the laboratory and it may be difficult for the experimenter to get them to do what she wants them to do.

2.  **Non-Experimental Methods**
    (i)   **Observation.** See Methods in Social Psychology page 73, ·
    (ii)  **Case Study.** The researcher builds up a detailed description of one individual. Freud built up such descriptions of his patients.
          **Disadvantages.** Case studies involve problems of subjectivity and uncontrolled variables. They only relate to one individual, therefore generalizations cannot be made.
          It is difficult for the researcher not to record an interpretation of what subjects say or do. If subjects are asked to talk about their past then it must be questioned whether memory is sufficiently reliable to give accurate details. Looking back on past events is called being **'retrospective'**.
    (iii) **Surveys.** See Methods in Social Psychology, page 72.

3.  **Clinical Interviews**
    Lengthy interviews are conducted in order to arrive at a detailed understanding of a person's mental processes. Piaget used this method in his studies of children's understanding.

## 4. Longitudinal and Cross Sectional Studies

When studying development, we are concerned with the change in people over time.

(a)  **A longitudinal study** involves repeated observations of the same individuals over an extended period of time.
     **Advantages.** Because individuals are compared with themselves at different points in time, subjects do not have to be matched over time.
     **Disadvantages.** Require much time from both subjects and researchers. Subjects may move away or in some other way drop out of the study.

(b)  **A Cross Sectional Study** compares groups of individuals at different ages at one point in time.
     **Advantages.** They are quicker and cheaper than longitudinal studies.
     **Disadvantages.** Measurements taken may not be valid if subjects differ on important variables other than age, e.g. educational background or health.

## 5. Correlational Studies

Correlation studies occur in both developmental and social psychology. However, it should be noted that correlation is not a method but a statistical technique. (See Drawing Conclusions from Data, page 103). A correlational study is not an experiment, no attempt is made to control or manipulate variables, it is the study of two or more naturally occurring events to analyse whether a relationship exists between these two events. The results of a correlational study do not imply a cause and effect relationship (no matter how high the correlation coefficient) because a third variable unknown to the researcher may be having an effect. For example if a researcher studies the number of storks entering a country in a year and the number of babies born, found there was a correlation between the two, this would only mean that a statistical relationship existed, not that storks were bringing babies.

## 6. Reliability, Validity and Standardization

Often in both developmental and social psychology, tests are developed and used to measure variables, e.g. intelligence tests or attitude scales.

A 'good' test must fulfil three criteria, i.e. it should be reliable, valid and standardized.

(a)  **Reliability.** This means that the test is consistent, i.e. it may be repeated with the same person to produce approximately the same result. There are several ways of checking this, one is called **Test-Retest method.** The test is performed twice with the same subjects. If there is a high correlation between the two sets of results the test can be said to be reliable.

29

(b)    **Validity.** A test is valid if it measures what it claims to measure. If a psychologist asked you to jump up and down to test your intelligence, you would question the **'face validity'** of the test.

(c)    **Standardization.** This refers to the establishment of a set of typical scores for the test (norms) against which other scores can be compared e.g. the mean (average) for an IQ test is usually 100, it is then possible to compare scores with this average score.

## PERCEPTUAL DEVELOPMENT

The term 'perception' often causes problems for students new to psychology. The process of dealing with information from the environment can be split into two separate processes.

**Reception** The process of tranduction of physical energy into nerve impulses. This takes place in receptors in sense organs (see pages 7-14).

**Perception** The organisation and interpretation of this information, which takes place in the brain. The interpretation of a stimulus depends upon i) the features of the stimulus itself, ii) the context in which it occurs and iii) past experience.

All sensory information is processed in this way, yet psychologists have concentrated their research on hearing (because of the importance of language to human beings) and seeing (because sight is our primary sense).

Do perceptual abilities develop as a result of genetic code or environmental stimulation? Psychologists have stumbled on considerable methodological limitations inherent in the study of such a concept. A rich variety of approaches has evolved. One of the limitations of this area of study is narrowing of the focus of research from perception in general to visual perception in particular.

1.   **Animal Studies**

The main methodological tool use in animal studies is **dark rearing** — a device considered by these psychologists to be ethically acceptable in non-human species. It consists of rearing animals from birth to maturity in darkness except for periods of controlled visual experience. It affords almost total control over environmental variables.

**Riesen (1950)** reared chimpanzes in total darkness (except for brief exposures to light whilst feeding) from birth to sixteen months old. On testing, they were found to have no startle reaction and appeared not to notice objects they did not touch. After five months exposure to normal light conditions, one animal gained these abilities but another, dark reared until thirty-one months old could not recover the decrements in its visual ability.

After studying similarly dark-reared chimps, **Weiskrantz (1956)** found that the retinas of such animals contained fewer and malformed cells. So it seems that the visual deficits found by Riesen were probably due to lack of development at a cellular level due to insufficient light stimulation.

Riesen repeated his first study with the exception that the chimp now wore a translucent mask for an hour or so per day, so that the diffused light would prevent retinal damage. On testing, this chimp also displayed disturbed and incomplete visual abilities, but quickly learnt visual-motor skills when exposed to a normal visual environment.

**Hubel and Wiesel (1963).** Two month old dark-reared kittens showed no electrical activity in cortical cells normally used to detect slope. It seems that the structures were lost during the period of deprivation and dis-use.

**Blakemore and Cooper (1966).** Dark-reared kittens were exposed daily to a visual environment consisting only of vertical lines. On testing, at maturity, the kittens
1.  had no startle reflex,
2.  had no visual placing response,
3.  would not follow a moving object unless it made a noise, and
4.  appeared to be blind to horizontal lines.

After a few days in a normal visual environment, the kittens had acquired 1,2 and 3 above, but never learned to respond to horizontal lines. At least three conclusions are possible from these results — (1) that line recognition develops through environmental stimulation, (2) the structures necessary for line recognition are present at birth but may degenerate with disuse and (3) the structures necessary for horizontal line recognition are taken over for use as, say, vertical line or slope detectors.

**Held and Hein (1965).** Held and Hein exposed pairs of dark-reared kittens to their famous 'kitten carousel' apparatus. After thirty hours exposure (three hours per day) the active kitten's visuo-motor abilities were normal, but the passive kitten lacked among other abilities, startle reaction and visual placing response. The passive kitten acquired these responses when exposed to a normal visual environment for a few hours. It seems that kittens learn such visuo-motor abilities very quickly through interaction with the environment.

**Discussion of animal studies**
1.  It is clear that the physiological development and/or maintenance of the visual system requires light stimulation. Maybe the effects of dark rear-

ing are greater at a certain age, in which case a critical or sensitive period is indicated.

2. A clear distinction must be made between perception (in general) and visuo-motor co-ordination (in particular). Blakemore's kittens showed a temporary deficit in visuo-motor co-ordination (also clearly shown by Held and Hein) *and* a permanent inability to react to horizontal lines.

3. Perception is not one process — it has many components and psychologists argue as to what should and should not be called 'perceptual process.' perception is also difficult to quantify and measure. When dealing with the possible perceptual processes we choose to attribute to non-human species we must remember to be cautious when generalising the results to human kind.

4. Complete development of visual abilities requires self-directed **interaction** with a rich and full visual environment.

## 2. Human Neonate Studies

To understand the developmental origins of human perception, we should study newly born humans. Certain methodological side steps must be made to avoid the problems of studying very young children, namely, lack of speech and the ethical restrictions on deprivation studies.

### R.L. Fantz: Development of the perception of form and pattern

Fantz pioneered the use of the **stimulus preference method** in an effort to determine whether the perception of pattern and form are present in very young infants. If a child possesses an ability at the age of say, one week old, there is a fair chance it was born with that ability. This is evidence in favour of a genetic basis for that ability. In his 1958 study he presented three black and white patterns in turn paired with a grey reference disc to thirty infants each week from their first to fifteenth week of age.

Fig 2.1

Each infant was laid on her back with the stimuli presented directly above her eyes. Fantz measured the length of time each baby looked at each pattern in the pair. It was found that the infants *did* respond differentially to the different patterns, but it is not possible to say whether the babies were responding to differences in brightness lines, angles or whatever.

In 1961 Fantz took fortynine infants aged four days to six months and presented them with all possible pairs of the stimuli in Fig.2.2.

**Fig. 2.2**

At all ages the infants looked most at the 'true face' and 'scrambled face' and hardly at all at stimulus 3. There was a very slight preference shown for the true face but this was not completely consistent, as the children aged 3½ months preferred the scrambled face! Such results need cautious interpretation, especially as these results have proved difficult to replicate, e.g. Hershenson (1964) found no preferences for the true face in infants aged two to four days. Hershenson did find however, that infants prefer medium brightness and **simple** chequerboard patterns.

**Discussion of stimulus preference method**
1. These results are difficult to interpret. What seems reasonably clear is that infants show preferences in the first week of life and we can infer from that that they can tell the difference between patterns. This does not support the 'blooming, buzzing confusion' idea and is worthy of comment.
2. Fantz did not use proper **scaling** procedures. In other words he could not quantify the precise differences between the stimuli he used. E.g. how do you quantify 'pattern', 'form' and 'complexity'?
3. In 1965, Haynes, White and Held found that the newborn is unable to adjust the focal length of her eye. This has implications for the studies so far described. Only a fraction of the subjects saw anything like a sharp image, the rest had various degrees of blurring.
4. Bower (1966) offers substantial criticism of the bodily position of the infants in Fantz's experiments, suggesting that when babies are placed on their backs on a flat surface 1) they are frightened and 2) their movements are restricted by their need to stop themselves rolling over sideways. Further, Bower suggests that unless the experimenter is vigilant the infant subject might drift off into a half asleep state with eyes open.

**T.R.G. Bower: Development of depth perception, shape and size constancy**

In 1970 Bower, Broughton and Moore demonstrated that ten day old babies live in a three dimensional world when the babies 'defended' themselves against both a real onrushing cube and a 'cube' image in a shadowcaster. This result has been confirmed and extended by Ball and Tronick (1971) who found that infants would defend themselves against a shadowcast image which appeared as though it would hit them, but not defend themselves against a similar image that appeared as though it would miss them.

Bower also investigated the acquisition of shape constancy — the tendency for the shape and identity of an **object** to be seen as the same regardless of changes in the shape and orientation of the **retinal image.** Using an instrumental conditioning procedure, he trained six week old infants to turn their heads to one side in the presence of stimulus A (Fig.2.3) in orientation 1. When subsequently tested, the infants had generalised their responses *only* to stimulus A in orientation 2, and not to stimulus B in orientations 1 and 2. This shows that they ignored retinal image changes and responded to similarities in object *shape* only.

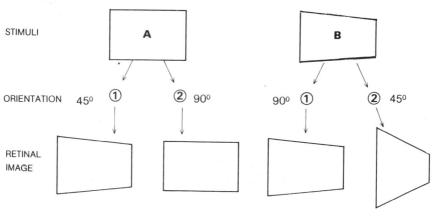

fig. 2.3.

Bower and Dunkeld (1978) suggested that shape constancy may be present in two week old infants by measuring 'defence' responses to rotating shadowcast stimuli. It seems as though young infants have a well defined notion of the relationship between object identity and shape changes.

Using a similar instrumental conditioning procedure, Bower (1966) demonstrated depth perception and size constancy in two week old infants. Size constancy is the tendency for the size of an *object* to be seen as the same regardless of changes in the size of the *retinal image.* This usually leaves the perceptual system no choice but to interpret retinal image size changes as an object of constant size moving towards or away from the observer.

He trained infants to turn their heads to one side in the presence of a 30cm cube at 1m distance. The infants generalised their responses to the other stimuli in the order most to least from left to right in Fig.2.4.

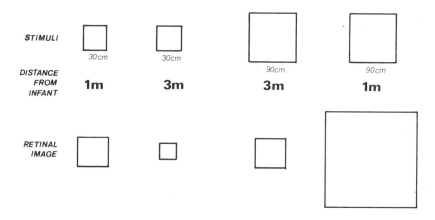

**Fig. 2.4**

So the infants paid attention to the *object* size regardless of retinal image size. This suggests that the infants do have size constancy.

**Discussion of Bower's Work**

1. Bower's results have proved to be difficult to repeat.
2. The instrumental conditioning method used by Bower is not direct evidence for shape or size constancy, since it is not possible to state exactly which elements of the stimulus the infant is generalising to.
3. The 'defence' response observed by Bower disappears as soon as the infant is laid on her back. No one can explain why, but this does raise questions about the usefulness of the response as a general measure of perceptual awareness.
4. Bower himself points out that simply because an infant cannot do something at say ten weeks old, that does not mean to say that newborns also cannot do it. E.g. newborn infants will perform a 'walking' motion if supported, whereas at ten weeks old they cannot perform this action under similar circumstances.
5. Given the problems in communication, arranging stimuli, bodily position, levels of consciousness, etc. Bower also warns us that the easiest thing to do is show that a very young human *cannot* do something.

## Gibson and Walk: Depth perception

In 1960 E.J. Gibson and R.D. Walk reported the development of their famous apparatus the 'visual cliff'. It's early applications with six month old humans, newborn goat kids and the like, told us only that if an animal is mobile (at whatever age) it can also see in depth. An hour or so observation in the farmyard would also have shown us that the newest of newborn foals, lambs or goat kids do not stand up and proceed to go around bumping into things.

The visual cliff is a very useful tool in evaluating the visual abilities of dark-reared animals and has been used to good effect in many of the experiments referred to on pages 30-32.

Gibson and Walk also used the visual cliff to investigate the acquisition and relative importance of pattern density and motion parallax in the depth perception of day-old chicks and dark-reared rats. To test pattern density only, a reduced pattern was placed immediately under the glass on the 'deep' side of the cliff and to test motion parallax only, a blown up pattern was placed on the floor of the 'deep' side of the cliff. Both the rats and the chicks used motion parallax but *not* pattern density.

More recently J. Campos (1978) measured a *decrease* in the heart rate of two month old infants when put on a visual cliff. He believed that this meant they could see the drop and were curious but not frightened (fear is usually indicated by an *increase* in heart rate) and that fear of drops is probably learned later.

## 3. Distortion and readjustment studies

One of the features of innate abilities is their inflexibility. Conversely, learned behaviour is flexible and adaptable — generally speaking, learning is reversible. In order to exploit this distinction, several psychologists have tried to reveal the capacity of the visual perceptual system to adapt to new situations. These new situations have included total inversion of the visual field (upside-down and back-to-front) colour distortion and prismatic distortion (prisms have a peculiar variable distorting effect on images).

In 1896 G.M. Stratton wore apparatus over one eye (with the other blindfolded) for eight days but the diary that he kept of his experiences is very difficult to interpret. Stratton undertook no controlled testing of his abilities from day to day. He reported that certain elements of the environment appeared the right way up if he could summon a strongly-held belief such as gravity acting downwards. The other 'adaption' seems to have been his motor-coordination coping better with an upside-down world, in other words while wearing the apparatus the world rarely if ever appeared the right way up.

P.H. Ewert (1930) use a binocular inverting apparatus and some controlled tests were performed involving manipulation of coloured blocks. The world did not turn the right way up for his subjects and this was born out by the tests, even after 14 days. He did find, however, considerable movement adaptation to the inverted world.

I. Kohler (1964) conducted a series of experiments, one involved an up-down inversion with no left-right inversion. His subjects were encouraged to practice motor tasks during the ten days of the experiment, and Kohler found substantial adaptation, at least to the extent that when the apparatus was removed the subjects sometimes saw objects as upside-down. It seems that the upside-down *and* left-right inversions in Stratton's and Ewert's experiments proved too much for the adaptive capacity of the human visual system.

## DEVELOPMENT OF THINKING

### 1.   The work of Jean Piaget (1896-1980)

Piaget's theory is sometimes described as **maturational** because he believed that the development of the intellect depends upon the development of the nervous system. Piaget maintained that the biological structure of the organism dictates they *way* the organism functions (the functions are unchanging or **invariant)** and these functions bring the organism into stylised contact with the environment leading to the development of cognitive structures (the structures are changeable or **variant).** So Piaget firmly believes in the *interaction* between maturation and environment being responsible for the development of intellect.

(a)   **Variant cognitive structures.** Piaget breaks the intellect down into two types of structure, schemata and operations. Both are open to change via interaction with the environment at any time.

A schema is the internal representation of a sequence of actions, and can be an inherited reflex such as sucking or visual searching (looking). As the infant gets older the simple schemata become extended through experience into more elaborate patterns of responses such as head turning, reaching etc. in anticipation of the nipple. In still older children, schemata shift from physical actions to mental actions.

Operations are more complex structures acquired in middle/late childhood and are reversible logical manoeuvres. E.g. the knowledge that subtraction will reverse or 'undo' addition.

(b)   **Invariant functions.** Schemata and operations are developed by interaction between the environment and the biological structure of the child. This interaction takes place because the child's behaviour is directed by the two functions — **organisation** and **adaptation.**

**Organisation** is the inborn tendency to co-ordinate the existing cognitive structures and combine them into more complex systems, such as looking + grasping + sucking when feeding from a bottle.

**Adaptation** is the inborn predisposition to strive for balance with the environment. It comprises **assimilation** and **accommodation.**

**Assimilation** is when a child **takes in** a new experience and fits it into her existing schemata. E.g. children of a certain age call all men 'Daddy'. The schema 'Daddy' has to assimilate (take in) many new situations.

**Accommodation** is complementary to assimilation — neither can exist without the other. It is the adjusting of an existing schema to fit in with the requirements of the environment. E.g. the 'Daddy' schema will soon become elaborate enough to discriminate between 'daddy' and 'other men'.

As the child experiences new situations and events she can either incorporate the event into already existing schemata (assimilation) or modify those schemata to respond to the demands of the new situation (accommodation). The child gradually tends towards a balance between the demands of the environment and her cognitive structure. Piaget called this balance **equilibrium.** Equilibrium is a temporary state because the environment is continually presenting the child with new events, situations and stimuli, causing the child to adapt through further assimilation and accommodation.

The continuing organisation and adaptation creates new schema out of old ones and increases the child's ability to interact with the world. Piaget traces the development of cognitive structures through a series of stages, starting with the child incapable of independent thought and reliant on motor activities at birth, and ending up with 'adult' thought capable of abstract logic.

Because all children have the same biological structure and the same (invariant) ways of interacting with the world through assimilation and accommodation, all children pass through these stages in the same order, though not necessarily at the same age. The ages given are therefore only approximate.

**Sensorimotor Stage 0-2 yr.** The child becomes able to distinguish herself from the environment, seeks and repeats satisfying events to do with her own body (primary circular reactions) and later, objects, e.g. shaking a rattle (secondary circular reactions). Between 8 and 12 months she gradually shows awareness of the permanence of objects by searching for hidden or partly hidden toys. Gradually the child shifts from being dependent upon action to being able to represent events which are not in her perceptual field at the time. She begins to internalize the world or as Piaget says, to *symbolize.*

**Preoperational Stage 2-6/7 yrs.** The child extends the use of symbolic thought into language and the development of imaginative play. The child is **egocentric** — unable to see the world from another point of view — she is unable to **de-centre** (with herself as the centre of the perceptual world). This limits the child's thinking in many ways;

(a) **Irreversibility:**          a four-year-old is asked: 'Do you have a sister?'
                                                                          She replies, 'Yes'
                                            'What is her name?' 'Jane,' she replies.
                                                  'Does Jane have a sister?' 'No.'

(b) **Centration:** the child focuses on one dimension of an object, saying that one ball of clay is bigger because it is longer. This demonstrates lack of **conservation,** e.g. when presented with two equal sized balls of clay, the preoperational child will choose one rolled out into a 'sausage' shape as the 'largest.' Conservation of many attributes of the physical world have been studied, including mass (above), number length, liquids and area. The age at which a child is able to conserve, varies for different characteristics.

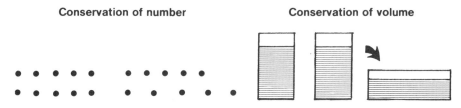

**Conservation of number**                    **Conservation of volume**

When one row of sweets is elongated         Though the volumes are equal, the
the preoperational child chooses the         properational child chooses the
bottom row as the one with the most sweets   tall vessel as the one with more liquid.

**Fig. 2.5**

**Concrete Operational Stage 6/7-11/12 yrs.** The child becomes less egocentric, and is able to take on the role of another. She is able to conserve mass, volume (liquid) number length etc., and shows increasing decentration. She also demonstrates the ability to use logical thought (Piaget calls **operations**) including the ideas of reversibility, classification (using classes and hierarchies) and seriation (putting things in an order e.g. of increasing height). *But,* the problems must involve real objects (Piaget says 'concrete' rather than 'real'). So a nine-year-old could only solve the problem: 'Jim is taller than Fred and Fred is taller than John, who is the tallest of the three?' if presented with named dolls to put in order.

39

**Formal Operational Stage 11/12 onwards.** The 'formal' in 'formal operational' means that the child can perform mental operations without recourse to real objects. The child can think abstractly and form (and test) hypotheses in her head. This greatly increases the flexibility of the intellect.

## 2. Impact of Piaget's Theory in the Classroom

Although Piaget himself was not mainly concerned with what goes on in schools, there are several general principles derived from his work which have guided eductional practice.

(a) Children are not 'miniature adults'. They are *qualitatively* different in their language and thought. Teachers must try and see things from the child's point of view.

(b) When working with Simon in Paris, Piaget learned more from the incorrect answers the children gave to his questions than the correct ones. He emphasised the importance of the 'clinical interview', in other words you learn more from talking through problems with children than by giving them tests which you simply mark 'right' or 'wrong'.

(c) Piaget believes that children learn through action and interaction with the environment. Having facts 'talked at' them does not stimulate the learning processes of children.

(d) In order for the processes of assimilation and accommodation to work best, children need new information and experiences to be *moderately* novel. If the new experience is too different it will not be assimilated and existing schemata will not be able to accommodate to it.

(e) Since children pass through the stages at different times and they acquire conservation of different attributes at different times, teaching mixed groups is not recommended. Individual work of the child's own choosing at the child's own pace is best.

These ideas will obviously clash with traditional methods of teaching, but many teachers have successfully incorporated some of these principles into their teaching practice.

## 3. Discussion of Piaget's Work

In recent years Piaget's theory was been criticised both generally and specifically.

1. Since the 1950's Piaget has been accused of vagueness in using terms such as 'schema', 'assimilation', 'accommodation' and 'equilibrium'. Although such terms have enabled Piaget to embrace a wide variety of thought processes, it has also made it difficult to test the theory with properly controlled experiments without stretching interpretations of particular terms. Thus, Bruner (1966) demonstrated that conservation responses in five, six and seven year-olds can be increased by getting the children to concentrate on verbal reasoning rather than the visual cues. However, closer inspection reveals that Bruner was using a much less strict criterion for conservation than Piaget.

2. Specific 'landmarks' in Piaget's theory such as object permanence and conservation have been investigated by a number of psychologists:

   Moore (1973) and Bower (1974) have refined the object permanence idea and shown that babies as young as four weeks old have some appreciation of the continued existence of objects out of sight. (This is much earlier than Piaget claims).

   McGarrigle and Donaldson (1974) were able to demonstrate conservation of number in four, five and six year-olds (theoretically, pre-operational children) by making a 'naughty teddy' responsible for the rearrangement of one line of sweets, rather than the experimenter. All other elements of the experimental situation were the same as Piaget's. Two issues arise from this and other experiments by Donaldson and her associates and Peter Bryant. Firstly, that the context in which the materials are presented is important. (In the 'naughty teddy' experiment, the children might have thought that simply because the adult experimenter had rearranged the sweets and then asked them a specific question, something *must* have changed). Secondly, perhaps Piaget overestimated the child's linguistic and memory abilities. Bryant suggests that Piaget's test situations make things as difficult as possible for the children and that with slight re-wording or a more real-life example children demonstrate reasonably sophisticated logical thought. (Remember Bower said that it is easy to show that a young child *cannot* do something).

   **N.B.** Piaget never spoke about the *ages* at which these landmarks must occur, simply that the *order* of events is unchangeable. No-one disputes that, e.g. object permanence and conservation are acquired at some age or other.

3. More substantial issues are raised by the work of Hughes (1975) and the suggestion by Donaldson that egocentricity is no more evident in preoperational children than adults. Egocentricity and the gradual

process of decentration are central to Piaget's explanation of preoperational thought. Hughes showed that three-and-a-half year olds could solve a 'boy hiding from a policeman' version of Piaget and Inhelder's 'mountains' task, suggesting that once again context and the relation to everyday life are important variables in childrens' thinking.

### 4. The Work of Jerome Bruner (1966)

Bruner also acknowledges that children's thought is different from adults, but he assigns less importance to the maturation of the nervous system and biological structure and more importance to the role of culture, language and play.

Bruner is concerned with the ways children internalize the world and their experiences in it. He believes that there are three types of internal **representation** of external events. These representations are *not* stages to be passed through, rather they are *ways* of storing and using information about the environment.

(a) **Enactive Representation.** This is the first way the child has of representing the world and it consists entirely of actions. An event must be muscular activity in order for a child to deal with it. E.g., when a child plays with a rattle, the shaking movement of her hand is the internal representation of the rattle, so to the child, the shaking *is* the rattle. If the rattle accidentally falls from the child's hands, she might continue to shake her hand demonstrating the way the movement dominates her perception, no *image* of the rattle is necessary. Enactive representation continues to be useful to adults e.g. we have a sort of 'muscle memory' for such skills as riding a bicycle and we use gestures to help explain the way a corkscrew works etc.

(b) **Iconic Representation.** This is the second method of internally representing environmental events, and is the 'second string' to the child's cognitive 'bow', i.e. enactive representation is still available and used by the child but now experiences can be internalized as *images*. These images are visual, auditory, olfactory and tactile 'likenesses' of environmental events and this form of representation has obvious advantages over enactive. Kuhlman (1960) showed that children who used iconic representation (imagers) were better than non-imagers at remembering arbitrary labels and the pictures they were attached to because the imagers could use both sources of information, the picture and the nonsense label. However, the same imaging children were worse than non-imagers at spotting what a number of pictures had in common, because they were tied to the visual image.

(c)  **Symbolic Representation.** Symbolic representation is not tied to an image, action, nor any restricted aspect of an environmental event. A symbol is something which *stands for* something else — a white bar on a red circle *stands for* 'no entry', a white dove *stands for* 'peace'. Human language is a collection of symbols in the form of words, phrases and sentences which we can use to describe, store and manipulate environmental events *internally* in the form of thought.

Bruner describes two ways of storing and organising information using symbols: **categorisation** and **hierarchies.**

Categorisation is the ability to recognise the common elements in a number of different objects or events. The word 'cars' defines such a category which includes hundreds of objects of different colours, shapes, makes, with different numbers of wheels and doors etc. The ability to categorise enables the child to shake off the limitations of the sensory information, and see also the common elements of the category.

Tulving and Pearlstone demonstrated the effectiveness of categorisation as an aid to thinking in a memory experiment. They asked subjects to memorize a list of words but then half the subjects were given a blank piece of paper to write the answers down and the rest were given a piece of paper with a number of categories printed on it, into which the memorized words fitted. The 'category' group recalled many more words than the group with the blank paper.

The formation of hierachies also helps in the organisation of information. G.H. Bower and others in 1969 conducted an experiment similar to Tulving and Pearlstone's, but instead of using categories, they used hierachies when the words were presented to the subjects. The group who were shown the hierachies recalled more than twice as many words than the non-hierarchy group.

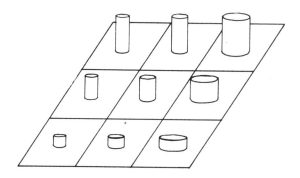

**Fig. 2.6**

The powerful combination of categorisation and hierarchies enables us to organise and manipulate the elements of the internal representation of a stimulus without the stimulus having to be present. Bruner and Kenny (1966) demonstrated the effectiveness of these aspects of symbolic representation. They used children aged between five and seven years, the younger ones using mainly iconic representation, the older ones able to use symbolic representation. Using the apparatus in Fig.2.6 the experimenter first removed a few glasses — all the children could successfully replace them and describe how the glasses were different. All the children could replace the glasses when the experimenter scrambled the array leaving glasses out of position. All of these tasks can be performed using the visual cues and iconic representation. When the experimenter removed all but on glass, changed its position on the grid and asked the children to remake the array around the remaining glass, children tied to the image in iconic representation could not perform the abstract manipulations of the array necessary to successfully replace the glasses; those able to use symbolic representation completed the task easily.

5.  **The Implications of Bruner's Work for Education**

    (a)  Bruner emphasises the separate development of language and thought, with language being ahead of thought up to the age of six or seven. Then we see the rapid development of symbolic representation as the combination of language and thought — thinking being given a boost by language.

    (b)  Before the interaction of language and thought at age 6/7 Bruner stresses the importance of action in cognitive development. The powerful influence of enactive representation means that action is an important factor — particularly *play*. Bruner does not think maturation is as important as learning, given the right environment and playthings. Sylva, Bruner and Genova (1976) demonstrated that the learning potential of play was equal to modelling when children were required to solve a simple problem.

    (c)  Bruner maintains that formal schooling (predominantly verbal and abstract reasoning) is probably in appropriate before the combination of language and thought.


**INTELLIGENCE**

There is no generally accepted definition of the term 'intelligence'. In 1904 A. Binet and T. Simon were asked by the school authorities in Paris to devise a method of picking out those children who would benefit from education and those who would not could be removed from traditional classes to relieve the overcrowding. Binet and Simon made some risky assumptions e.g. that if the children had equal educational experience and equal opportunities to learn, those that showed better skills and general knowledge were showing greater intellectual ability.

Also many of the questions in the test that they devised involved skills taught in school so they were using academic achievement to predict future academic achievement. This is a **screening** procedure working on the idea that if you are good at something *now* you are likely to be good at it in the future. Those children that did not do well on the day of the test were assumed to be a bad bet for doing well in the future.

A further assumption is that intelligence tests measure an underlying *capacity* to succeed in the educational system, but in this respect intelligence is like learning and can never be directly observed or measured (see learning and performance p. 27). Intelligence can only be measured along with *performance*. In other words, there may be many reasons for a final mark on an intelligence test which have nothing to do with the assumed underlying capacity — maybe the child was feeling unwell at the time etc.

Binet introduced the idea of 'mental age'. He believed that intellectual capacity increased with age. A German psychologist, W. Stern, devised the Intelligence Quotient or I.Q. (see p. 94) and L.M. Terman, the man who introduced intelligence testing to the U.S.A., assumed that this capacity to learn would remain stable over time i.e. the I.Q. of a person would not change as they got older. The experimental investigation of this assumption has proved very difficult because (1) it is difficult to assess the ability of very young children and (2) it assumes a continuity between the intellectual functionings of children and adults. Piaget and Bruner have demonstrated that children are definitely *not* miniature adults when it comes to thinking so maybe a measure made during childhood is not a good predicter of adult abilities. McCall and others (1973) used many I.Q. tests and measures of infant performance on children aged between 2½ and 17 years old. It was a longitudinal study in which 33% of the subjects showed a change of over 30 I.Q. points and the largest change was of 74 points. The high I.Q. children showed greater changes than low I.Q. children.

Binet believed that the distribution of intelligence throughout the population would be 'normal' (see p. 101). In fact if it didn't show a normal distribution he simply eliminated the questions that caused it to deviate. Statistically speaking, it is reasonable to assume that intelligence is normally distributed since we assume that a person's I.Q. is the result of many factors all acting at random. (See reliability, validity and standardisation p. 29).

## 1. Intelligence and Culture

The role of intelligence testing in screening for academic achievement has recently been criticised on the basis that the tests are **culture-bound**: i.e., the tests reflect white middle-class culture, language and values. This is only to be expected since the tests were designed to measure and predict achievement in a white middle-class educational system. Although attempts have been made, it is not possible to construct a 'culture-free' or 'culture-fair' test. All tests discriminate against the 'culturally deprived' individuals and groups, as does the educational system as a whole, especially when ethnic groups with certain cultural backgrounds do not understand the western idea of 'schooling', with teachers talking about objects and events not present in the the classroom and even things that have never existed, and all in a context of white technological supremacy.

## 2. The Nature-nurture Debate on Intelligence

There are several sources of data to fuel the nature-nurture debate on intelligence, some collected under dubious circumstances and much of it contradictory.

Hebb (1949) tried to clarify the situation by suggesting that there are two types of intelligence:

(i)  **Intelligence A** is the individual's **potential** intelligence made possible by their genetically determined biological structure. Exactly how much of this potential is realised depends upon the influence of the environment.

(ii) **Intelligence B** is the amount of intelligence A that is realised by interaction with the environment. Factors such as nutrition, child rearing practices, culture and education exert their influence on the amount of intelligence that is expressed.

Realising the importance of the operational definition of intelligence — 'intelligence is what is measured by intelligence tests' — and the relationship between performance and intelligence, Vernon proposed a third type of intelligence: **intelligence C**. Intelligence C is the amount of intelligence B that is sampled by intelligence tests. Only intelligence C can be directly measured, and since it is circularly defined it does not help us sort out the tangle of variables which contribute to an individual's I.Q.

## 3. Family Studies and Twin Studies

The idea behind family studies is to discover any relationship between genetic similarity and trait similarity, the trait in question being intelligence. Genetic similarity between humans can vary between monozygotic (identical) twins and totally unrelated strangers, and a correlation analysis is used to determine the strength of relationship between intelligence of each individual in pairs of specially selected subjects.

Many of the studies concentrate on pairs of twins; since identical twins have identical genes, any differences between them are due to the effects of the environment. Similarly it is argued that fraternal twins reared together have different genes but the same environment, so differences between them must be due to the genetic differences. In Fig.2.7 are the results of some of the best known family and twin studies expressed as correlation coefficients (see p. 29 and 103).

| | | A<br>Burt<br>(1953) | B<br>Newman<br>Freeman and<br>Holzinger<br>(1928) | C<br>Shields<br>(1962) | |
|---|---|---|---|---|---|
| 1 | Monozygotic twins; reared together | .92 | .91 | .76 | |
| 2 | Monozygotic twins; reared apart | .84 | .67 | .77 | |
| 3 | Dizygotic twins; reared together | .53 | .64 | | |
| 4 | Dizygotic twins; reared apart | | | .57 | |
| 5 | Siblings; reared together | .49 | | | |
| | | D<br>Snygg<br>1938 | E<br>Jensen<br>1969 + 1973 | F<br>Skodak +<br>Skeels<br>1949 | H<br>Erlenmeyer-<br>Kimling and<br>Jarvik 1963<br>approximate<br>figures |
| 6 | Parents paired with children | | | | .52 |
| 7 | Adopted children paired with natural parents | .13 | .50 | .44 | |
| 8 | Adopted children paired with adoptive parents | | .20 | | |
| 9 | Aunts-Uncles-Nieces-Nephews | | .34 | | |
| 10 | Siblings reared together | | .55 | | .49 |
| 11 | Siblings reared apart | | | | .46 |
| 12 | Unrelated people reared together | | | | .24 |
| 13 | Unrelated people reared apart | | − 0.01 | | 0.00 |

**Fig.2.7**

Despite the apparent wealth of studies, the results are at best unclear and sometimes contradictory. The higher the correlation coefficient, the greater the similarity between the intelligence of both members of the pair. Generally speaking the results suggest that there is a reasonably strong genetic component to I.Q. since the I.Q.'s of monozygotic twins are more similar than those of dizygotic twins even when the MZ twins are reared apart and the DZ twins reared together (rows 1-4 columns A-C Fig.2.7). Also, children are more similar to their biological parents in I.Q. (whether living together or apart) than to their adopted parents. However, this does not mean that the environment has no influence at all. Far from it in fact if we inspect Snygg's result and columns E and H rows 12 and 13, an environmental effect is evident (Fig.2.7).

4.   **Criticism of Twin Studies**

(a)   It is very difficult to identify identical twins, and some studies may have made mistakes, both including 'non-identical' twins in the sample of 'identical' twins and vice-versa.

(b)   It has recently been confirmed that there are genetic differences even between identical twins, and though small, it does add error to the results.

(c)   It is assumed in twin studies that when twins are reared together, the environment is the same for both. This is not the case in many families where, in an effort to impart and maintain each twin's separate identity, each twin is treated differently.

(d)   The samples of twins used in these studies are small, leaving room for a large statistical error.

(e)   It now seems highly likely that Burt made up his twin studies results so that they fitted in with his own ideas on intelligence and heredity.

5.   **The Effects of a 'Good' Environment**
   Some studies have investigated the effects of changing the environment on the I.Q.'s of groups of subjects, usually children.
   **Skeels (1966).** Skeels found that the I.Q.'s of 13 nineteen-month old orphans increased over 28 points 1½ years after they were transferred from an overcrowded orphanage to an environment where they were given a greater amount of individual attention by young girls acting as 'substitute mothers'. Twelve 19 month old orphans in a control group left at the overcrowded orphanage *lost* up to 26 I.Q. points. The effects were still evident 2½ years later and the differences were maintained into adulthood, when Skeels measured the I.Q.'s of the two groups twenty-one years later. Similar im-

provements have been noted by Clarke and Clarke (1954) in subnormal adults when moved to a more favourable environment.

Curiously, I.Q. tests and results may themselves constitute part of the environment which can disadvantage a child. Mercer (1972) alerted psychologists to the destructive effect of labelling a child as 'retarded' or 'low ability'. Such labelling influences the schooling a child receives — although ostensibly more 'appropriate', sometimes such establishments are places where low motivation and lack of stimulation become institutionalised, e.g. secondary modern schools.

Labelling also influences the attitudes of others and, most important, can lead to a low self concept.

## THE DEVELOPMENT OF LANGUAGE AND COMMUNICATION

Young children pass through several stages of language development.

(a) **Babbling.** By 3 months children engage in conversational babbling. During the babbling stage, the basic sounds of language, called **phonemes,** begin to emerge. Also, the child from 6 to 12 months produces a full range of exotic sounds which could be applicable to most languages, but gradually these sounds become narrowed down to those sounds that are used in the language which is being spoken around the child.

(b) **Utterance of single words.** In nearly all cultures a child's first communications consist of single words, (often 'Mama' or 'Papa').

(c) **Utterance of two words together.** By the age of 2 years most children are producing two-word sentences usually consisting of a noun and a verb, e.g. 'me go'.

The list of words whose meaning the child understands, **vocabulary,** multiplies 200 to 300 times during the second year of life. The learning and understanding of the meaning of words and phrases is called **semantics.** The child must also learn the way in which words are put together to form phrases and sentences, i.e. grammar. This is known as **syntax.** Grammar also consists of forming the plurals of words and putting verbs into different tenses. This is known as **morphology.**

### 1. The Learning of Language

(a) **Skinner's View.** Skinner thought that language learning could be explained in terms of instrumental conditioning techniques, e.g.

49

reinforcement and shaping (see instrumental conditioning p. 21).
Rheingold, Gewirtz and Ross (1959) observed 3 month old infants over six days.

Days 1 and 2 — The frequency of the infants spontaneous vocalizations were recorded. A woman periodically looked over the crib.

Days 3 and 4 — Vocalizations were rewarded. The woman smiled, made sounds and stroked the child whenever she made sounds.

Days 5 and 6 — The woman once more became unresponsive — extinction period.

**Results.** Vocaliazations increased on days 3 and 4 when rewards were given and declined on days 5 and 6.

However, although this indicates that language can be learned by reinforcement, it does not mean that language is learnt this way in the natural environment.

Skinner has argued that through reinforcement, young children learn the basis of grammar. Studies tend to contradict this.

Brown, Cazden and Bellugi (1967), Brown and Hanlon (1970) conducted observation studies of children learning to speak. It was found that it was not grammar that motivated parents to respond positively or negatively but factual inaccuracies, truth, insults or foolishness.

(b)   **Observational Learning.** many early researches assumed that imitation played a large part in language learning. That is, a child exposed to a model producing language would automatically pick up that language.

Cazden (1965) worked for three months with 2 groups of children.

Group 1 — simply talked with the experimenter, who took care not to repeat the child's words or phrases.

Group 2 — the experimenter repeated and placed in proper grammatical form, all the childrens' utterances.

**Results.** A much greater improvement on a variety of linguistic tests was found among Group 1 — the children who simply conversed.

The results indicate that children do not learn to speak properly by imitating adult utterances, or children would have picked up 'proper' speech in Group 2 and shown this in the tests.

However, despite these studies both reinforcement and imitation must contribute in some way to language acquisition, e.g. children pick up accents by imitation. Although they alone do not account for language development, they do exert some influence, in the same way that they influence most processes of learning.

(c) **Biological View.** Some researchers propose that humans are uniquely pre-disposed to language and that knowledge of language is innate, e.g. Chomsky. This belief is encouraged because:

(a) humans have a unique, finely tuned vocal apparatus;

(b) the left hemisphere of the human brain has an area specifically devoted to language mastery (see also cerebral cortex p.6).

(c) Lenneberg (1967), for example, believes that the development of language depends on a critical period and language must be mastered during the first decade of life or it will never develop at all.

There is little doubt that children learn grammar quickly and can extract the underlying rules of language and apply them in new situations. Chomsky believes that children enter the world equipped with an innate Language Acquisition Device (L.A.D.) responsible for the acquisition, understanding and use of language. Chomsky proposes that children are biologically programmed to acquire a finite number of grammar rules and from these rules they can then generate an infinite number of grammatically correct sentences.

Critics of this view propose that if this was the case language learning would not be subject to gradual acquisition, errors, inappropriate use and the problems most school children have mastering plurals, tenses, adjectives, adverbs etc. Also children who can get what they want or solve problems without using language are likely to be slow in the development of language. This also applies to twins who communicate non-verbally or children who have parents who encourage 'baby talk'.

Thus the differences between individual children, although not disproving the biological point of view, do point to the importance of psychological and social factors.

(d) **Animal Studies.** In the last twenty years animal studies have suggested that non-human primates may also have the capacity for language development.

(i) **Gardner and Gardner.** Taught a chimp, named Washoe, American sign language (Ameslan). They used the processes of imitation, reinforcement and chatting with her, starting from when she was a year old. At about 4 years of age Washoe was using 85 different signs with the correct meaning and at 5 years of age she was using 160 signs. She also *produced* strings of signs, initiated communications and was able to communicate meaningfully with her trainers.

In 1970 Washoe went to Roger Fonts in Oklahoma who was conducting extensive research with other chimps using Ameslan.

51

He has found:

1) That the chimps used Ameslan among themselves even when no human was present;

2) Chimps could invent names for objects — one chimp, Lucy, responded to a watermelon with the sign 'fruit drink';

3) Chimps can learn signs from one another.

(ii) **Duane Rumbaugh.** He studied Lana, a chimp who lived with a computer. If she pushed the correct buttons with signs on them in the correct order the computer would give her what she wanted, e.g. if she pressed 'Please machine, give piece of chocolate, full stop', the machine would give her a piece of chocolate.

(iii) **David Premack.** He worked with a mature, caged, female chimp, Sarah. He used plastic tokens varying in size, shape, colour and texture as 'words', and shaped Sarah's learning of words and sentences with food as reinforcement. She developed an understanding of words, sentences, questions, negatives and conditional phrases.

However, without reinforcement, Sarah did not show any interest in language; she practically never initiated communication and when the tokens were left lying in her cage she generally ignored them. In this respect she was unlike Washoe and Fonts' chimps.

So the studies indicate that non-human primates are capable of some form of language and humans may not be unique in this respect.

2. **The Nature/Nurture Debate and Language.** Again the dispute between the biological arguments for the development of language and the environmental arguments is disregarded in favour of the view that language develops as interaction between biological heritage and environmental influences.

# 3

# SOCIAL EMOTIONAL DEVELOPMENT

## EARLY EXPERIENCE

Newborn children are helpless and need an older person to care for them; this person may not necessarily be the mother and may be referred to as the caretaker.

A child forms a bond of attachment with its caretaker which usually becomes firmly established by the time the child reaches 8 or 9 months of age. Although attachment is still being researched, it is thought that it takes the form of staying close to the adult and showing distress on separation. The adult also forms a strong attachment to the infant and tries to keep them close.

One of the important aspects of the study of the attachment bond is its consequences for the person later in life.

To study the attachment bond both animal and human studies have been carried out.

## ANIMAL STUDIES

(a) **Imprinting.** Imprinting refers to the process by which new born animals and birds form a relatively permanent bond with the parent in a comparatively brief period of time.

(b) **Konrad Lorenz.** Lorenz observed that goslings began to follow their mother almost immediately after hatching. The bond seemed to help the mother train and protect her offspring. Lorenz found that if he kept goslings with him during the first 24 hours after hatching they would follow him and not another goose. He also found that if he took a group of goslings that had been imprinted on him and a group that had been imprinted on the mother, mixed them together and placed the group under a box, then when the box was lifted, those imprinted on Lorenz followed him and those imprinted on the mother followed her. Lorenz therefore established that this following response let to the formation of an attachment. Lorenz did many experiments on imprinting, for example, he imprinted jackdaws on himself and eventually the mature jackdaws attempted to mate with him. Lorenz concluding that imprinting could influence sexual preference.

Lorenz proposed that the time during which imprinting could take place was genetically determined; if it did not occur in this time then it never would, he called this the **critical period**. He also believed that once imprinting had occured the attachment was irreversible.

(c) **Hess (1972)** did many experiments in the laboratory imprinting ducks on decoys, flashing lights, toys etc. He proposed that the strengh of the bond varies and seems to depend on the activity of the duckling and the type of stimulus. He believed that the effort expended in following e.g. if the bird had difficulty following the imprinting stimulus, strengthened the bond: Hess (1958). He also proposed that in ducks the imprinting response, although it could occur as early as one hour after hatching, was at its strongest between 12 and 17 hours after hatching and that after 32 hours the response was unlikely to occur at all. Thus Hess supported the idea of the critical period.

Hess also proposed that the critical period depended on two growth processes. Imprinting cannot occur until the bird is strong enough to get up and move around, but it must occur before it has developed a strong fear of large moving objects.

(d) **Guiton 1959.** He established that chicks reared in isolation remained capable of being imprinted on moving objects after the critical period was supposed to have ended. He proposed that environmental factors influence the duration of the period during which imprinting may take place and therefore some researchers do not see the length of time as so critical and prefer to refer to it as the **sensitive period**. He also found that cockerels which he imprinted on a pair of yellow gloves but which he later introduced to other ducks showed normal sexual preferences, thus indicating that imprinting may be reversed or changed, again indicating that sensitive period may be a better description than critical period.

(e) **Sluckin 1961 and Bateson 1964.** They also found that if ducklings were kept in social isolation the imprinting period could be extended.

## ATTACHMENT IN MONKEYS

In the same way that Lorenz proposed that the gosling must imprint on its mother within the critical period, Harlow (1962) has contended that monkeys must form their attachments during the first year of life.

His experiments took several forms:

1. Infant monkeys reared in isolation - some died, others were frightened and behaved in an abnormal manner, failed to interact normally with other monkeys when older.

2. Infant monkeys reared with surrogate mothers - either bare wire mothers or wire mothers covered with soft cloth. Regardless of which surrogate mother had the feeding bottle attached to it all the monkeys preferred the 'soft' mother and clung to it. They formed a bond with the cloth mother.

   Monkeys with the cloth mother did not show the fearful and neurotic behaviour of the completely isolated monkeys but they failed to develop normally, in that when older they had difficulty establishing peer relationships, problems engaging in sexual activity and made poor parents.

Harlow also showed that there is a critical/sensitive period for the development of infant monkey attachment. Monkeys isolated for the first 8 months of life had difficulty in later establishing an attraction to the 'cloth mother'. They derived little assurance from it when in stressful situations. They also lost whatever attraction they had acquired for the cloth surrogate mother if separated from her.

**Criticisms and later studies.** Recently other researchers have challenged Harlow's original view that mothering is central to normal development in all primates.

One group of infant monkeys reared without a mother or surrogate mother, but with peers developed normally, Harlow & Harlow (1969). Harlow and Novak (1975) isolated four infant monkeys for a full year then allowed the isolated monkeys to look at one another and then at non-isolated monkeys. They then let the isolated monkeys play together and introduced them to normal younger infants to play with. Increasingly their behaviour began to resemble that of normal monkeys. Novak & Harlow (1975), as a result, suggest that a mother is not essential during infancy and that there is no strict critical period determining social development.

## ATTACHMENT IN HUMANS

It is difficult to generalize the results from studies of monkeys to humans.

In the late 1940's John Bowlby began to study the effects on children of separation from their mothers in early childhood. Various other studies followed.

(a)  **Goldfarb 1943** studied 15 boys and girls, ten to fourteen years old, who had been in an institution from a few months until about 3 years of age.

They were compared with 15 children brought up in foster homes. It was proposed that detrimental effects of institutionalized upbringing were apparent in almost every aspect of intellectual and social development.

(b)  **Bowlby 1944** studied 44 juvenile thieves and reported that, compared with a control group, they had certain personality traits typical of those deprived in childhood of maternal care and affection.

In 1951 Bowlby and his colleagues issued a report stating that infants suffer severely when in institutions that do not provide adequate care and normal infants, who had been separated prematurely from their mothers, suffered in terms of relating to people, playing and exploring.

From studies of children in hospital and in residential nurseries it was established that children under 5 years separated from their mother underwent the following reactions.

(i)   In approximately the first week they cried and displayed anger, i.e. protested.

(ii)  Then they cried intermittently but became quieter, i.e. despair.

(iii) After this they became more cheerful but appeared to have no preferences among their caretakers, i.e. emotionally detached. This was generally termed 'separation anxiety'.

Bowlby believed there existed a sensitive period in which babies form a bond of attachment with a caretaker (as with the ethologists and their ideas about imprinting). He felt that children who did not experience a close, warm and continuous relationship with the mother would suffer subsequent difficulties in development, emotionally and socially.

### Criticisms of Separation Studies

**Goldfarb study.** The control group and the experimental group may not have been equivalent and there was no control over the composition of each group.

**Bowlby 1944:** In a study of juvenile thieves Bowlby did not have a control group to enable him to compare how many non-delinquents had experienced separation.

**Freud and Dann (1951)** studied 6 children of pre-school age who had lost their parents in concentration camps but who had remained together as a group despite having themselves been in a camp and moved several times before they eventually ended up in an English nursery. Although the children did have emotional problems there was no evidence of gross disturbance; the strong ties and love which they had developed for each other appeared to have protected them, thus sustaining Harlow and Novak's (1975) conclusions on the presence of age mates.

**Rutter (1972)** studied a group of nine to twelve year old children living on the Isle of Wight, and a group of London children who had one or both parents who had been under psychiatric care. He found that although parental death may be followed by some disorder, delinquency is mainly associated with separation which follows parental discord. It is the unhappiness prior to, for example, a divorce, rather than the break itself which has the influence. Also suggests that the longer the disharmony lasts the greater the risk. Rutter (1972) summarizes the following hypotheses:-

(i)     Acute distress is probably due in part to the disruption of bonding with a permanent caretaker.

(ii)    Developmental retardation and intellectual impairment are consequences of privation of perceptual and linguistic experience.

(iii)   Dwarfism is usually due to nutritional privation.

(iv)    Enuresis is sometimes a result of stressful experiences.

(v)     Delinquency follows family discord.

(vi)    Psychopathy may be the end product of a failure to develop bonds of attachments in the first three years of life.

He also points out that as well as love and family relationships other factors in the environment greatly influence a child's development and that individual children respond differently in different situations.

**Patricia Morgan 1975** criticizes Bowlby and others for their emphasis on the 'mother' and maternal deprivation and assumptions that no other person is sufficient to care for the child.

Finally many of the studies in the area suffer from methodological problems. They are either, correlational studies (Rutter), case studies (Freud and Dann), observational studies involving interviewing etc. (Bowlby), or are unable to randomly select subjects for study and can have no influence over their differing previous experiences (see methods in Social and Developmental Psychology).

## CROSS CULTURAL STUDIES OF ATTACHMENT

(a) **Israel.** In a kibbutzim in Israel children are reared together under the care of a 'metapelet' who changes from time to time and they go and stay with their parents at weekends. The greatest attachment still seems to be towards the parents but it is proposed that their attachment behaviour and anxiety reactions are less intense than those of home reared children.

(b) . **East Africa.** Herbert and Gloria Leiderman (1974) worked in an East African agricultural village and compared infants raised in two kinds of homes.
Monomatric — single mother
Polymatric - many mothers
They found that the caretaking arrangements did not seriously affect the children.

## SOCIALISATION

**Learning Theory Approach to the acquisition of social behaviour.**

The Learning Theory Approach to the acquisition of behaviour is closely related to the work of Skinner and theories of reinforcement (see Instrumental Conditioning (p21). Experiments were performed and it was found that reinforcement, e.g. smiling, saying something nice, could influence a child's behaviour. Non-reinforcement could serve to extinguish previously reinforced behaviour and it was thought that by the use of schedules of reinforcement and shaping techniques a child's behaviour could be modified.

However, there were criticisms of this, in that behaviour had to first be performed before it could be reinforced; how did new pieces of behaviour occur? Also it was proposed that it was possible for children to learn actions without being reinforced.

**Social Learning Theory.**

Social learning theorists have attempted to enlarge the scope of learning theory and they have emphasized the importance of **observational learning and imitation** as well as **reinforcement.**

**Bandura and Walters 1963.** Typically children were allowed to watch a live or filmed **model** where the hero would repeatedly knock down an inflated rubber doll called a Bobo doll. The children were then left individually in a room with toys and a doll and their behaviour observed. The group that had observed the model copied many of his aggressive acts whereas those who had not seen the adult demonstrated notably fewer aggressive acts.

**Discussion Point 1.** Children who saw the model were copying, i.e. imitating his behaviour simply from having observed his behaviour.

**Bandrua, Ross and Ross (1965)** The experiment was similar to the previous one, however there were 3 groups of children.

Group A saw a final scene in which the model was rewarded for his aggressive acts.

Group B saw a final scene in which the model was punished for his aggressive behaviour.

Group C saw only the basic film and did not see the model being either rewarded or punished.

Children were then tested individually in a room containing the doll and other toys.

**Result.** When rewards were offered for copying aggressive acts all three groups A, B & C performed approximately the same number of acts.

Group A and Group C on average made the same number of aggressive acts.

Next the experimenters informed children that they would be rewarded each time they copied the aggressive acts of the model.

**Result.**When rewards were offered for copying aggressive acts all three groups A, B & C performed approximately the same number of acts.

**Discussion Point 2.** Although in the first part of the experiment Group B did not perform as many aggressive acts, when offered a reward they showed they had learnt (acquired) as many aggressive acts as the other 2 groups, showing that a child can learn something through observation without necessarily having to imitate that behaviour - this is the distinction between learning and performance. (see also Learning and Performance page 27).

If imitative behaviour is reinforced then that imitative behaviour will be continued, but even without reinforcement children will still imitate.

**Identification.** This is the process by which the child adopts the values, attitudes and behaviours of other people in order to be like them. e.g. A 2 year old little girl may want to be like mummy and therefore copies all mummy's actions. As she grows older these simple imitated attitudes and behaviours become part of her personality and what was imitation at age 2 becomes a well established set of ideas and behaviours at age 5. i.e. children imitate the behaviour of a person they identify with.

Identification is important in the development of sex roles and conscience.

(i) **Freud.** Freud's psychoanalytic theory (see page 60) holds that during the fourth and fifth years of life (the phallic stage) all children develop an unconscious wish to possess the opposite sexed parent and to do this they desire to do away with the same sexed parent. This in boys is called the oedipus complex, referring to the Greek myth in which Oedipus unwittingly kills his father and marries his mother.

The child's first important love object is his mother; his love gradually becomes erotically tinged and he wishes to sexually possess her. However, his father is an obstacle to this becoming the boy's rival, whom he wishes to do away with. However the boy is afraid his father will retaliate and having observed that women lack penises he is afraid that this retaliation may take the form of castration. This castration anxiety forces the boy to give up his incestuous feelings for his mother and defensively identify with his father, i.e. he imagines he can obtain some of the pleasure of possessing his mother indirectly by becoming like her lover, his father.

The boy therefore adopts his father's behaviours, attitudes and values.

The female version of the Oedipus complex is ill-defined and disputed by many psychologists, it is called the Electra complex and involves penis envy leading to identification with the mother.

(ii)  **Status Envy Theory J.W.M. Whiting 1960.** Whiting sees the young child struck by the parent's resources e.g. power, skills, knowledge, possession of the opposite sexed parent and he envies these. Hoping eventually to have the same privileges, the child assumes the characteristics of the adult, i.e. identifies with the adult.

An experiment by Bandura, Ross and Ross shows this. Two adults A and B are observed by a group of children. Adult A has possession of some toys and he gives some of these to adult B. Both adults then play with the toys in distinctively different ways.

The children who observed the behaviours imitated both adult A's behaviour and adult B's behaviour, but they imitated more of adult A's behaviour: i.e. both possession of resources (adult B) and control over resources (adult A) are strong motivators for imitation, but control over resources would appear to be the most important of the two factors.

(iii)  **Freud's Psychoanalytic Theory of Personality Development.** Sigmund Freud (1856-1939) lived during victorian times and his theory thus reflects the oppressive moral atmosphere of those times and the feeling that sexual desires should be kept hidden. He developed his theory through case studies, relying on his and other's recollections of childhood. He believed that childhood was extremely important in the formation of adult personality. According to Freud the personality develops in several psychosexual stages and sexual energy or libido governs important behaviours throughout life.

1. **The oral stage** (1st year) The child obtains gratification by stimulation through the mouth, putting things in the mouth or biting.

    Conflict or frustration at this stage may result in the adult being overly dependent on others or aggressive in terms of being very sarcastic or cynical.

2. **Anal stage** (2 - 3 years) The child obtains gratification by elimination or retention of faeces.

    Conflict or frustration at this stage may result in an adult who is messy or wasteful or an adult who is stingy and preoccupied with cleanliness, order and the possession of goods.

3. **Phallic stage** (4 - 6 years) The child obtains gratification through manipulation and stimulation of the genitals.

    The oedipus and electra complexes occur during this stage.

    Lack of identification with same sex parent may result in the development of homosexuality.

4. **Latent stage** (6 - 12 years) The libido does not focus on any bodily area.

5. **Genital stage** (Adolescence to adulthood). The libido is focused on the genitals and is directed towards heterosexual pleasure.

As the person passes through the stages, three underlying structures of the personality emerge - the **id, ego and superego.**

Freud proposed that at birth the personality consists exclusively of the id whose function is to gratify the instincts and is governed by the desire for pleasure.

However, regardless of how quickly the infant's needs are gratified during the oral stage, there will still be some delay and the child will have to realize that there is an external world. This realization leads to the development of the ego. The ego is characterised by realistic thinking and problem solving. The ego can therefore deal with a delay of gratification (pleasure). During the phallic stage the child experiences the oedipus or electra complex and the superego or conscience begins to develop when children identify with the same sex parent, adopting their attitudes and values.

**Criticisms of Freud's Theory**

1.  Freud used case studies from which generalization is not possible.

2.  His sample of subjects was biased (i.e. middle class, repressed women).

3.  He used the childhood recollections of people which may not have been accurate.

4.  It is very difficult to test Freud's theory by experimentation because Freud used unexplained and imprecise concepts.

5.  Observer bias may have unintentionally have effected his recording of subjects' recollections.

6.  There is very little scientific support for Freud's stages of development or his concepts of id, ego and superego.

## MORAL DEVELOPMENT

Theories of moral development have been put forward by Kohlberg, Piaget and Freud.

1.  **Lawrence Kohlberg.**
His theory focuses on the reasoning of an individual confronted by a moral or ethical dilemma. Usually his procedures involved posing a moral dilemma and then asking subjects to indicate how the main character should act and to provide a justification for that action. He distinguished three broad levels of moral development which each contain two stages.

### LEVEL 1
**Preconventional Level of Morality.** Right and wrong is dictated by standards outside the person without regard to their meaning; people behave in certain ways in order to avoid punishment.
**Stage 1. Punishment and obedience orientation.** Whether an action will be punished determines its goodness and badness and people obey rules in order to avoid punishment.
**Stage 2. Naive instrumental hedonism.** Actions are performed in order to obtain rewards or favours.

## LEVEL 2.
**Conventional Level of Morality.** People behave in ways which uphold the views of society and identify with members of society.

**Stage 3. Good-boy morality.** Actions are seen as good if they are well-intentioned and are accepted as such by others.

**Stage 4. Authority-maintaining morality.** This stage is characterized by a respect for authority, a belief that rules of society are right and a desire to avoid the disapproval of authority.

## LEVEL 3
**Morality of self-accepted moral principles.** The person defines her own values and principles and conscience guides actions.

**Stage 5. Morality of individual rights, contract and democratically accepted laws.** Right action is defined in terms of standards and individual rights. Community welfare is important.

**Stage 6. Morality of individual principles of conscience.** Principles are self-chosen and these dictate actions.

Kohlberg claims

(a)  that these stages are universal and fixed.

(b)  that everyone must pass through the same stages in the same order, although ages for each stage vary among subjects. Kohlberg's studies have shown that typically children in middle childhood are pre-conventional, young adolescents (13 - 16 years) are at the conventional level and older adolescents are at the level of self-accepted moral principles. It has also been shown that the stages and sequences are the same in certain other cultures (Kohlberg 1969).

### Criticisms of Kohlberg's Theory.

(i)  The morals of other cultures may be different and based on different ideas to those held by western society, therefore the theory and measures may not be applicable to all other societies.

(ii)  What a person says she would do in a certain situation may bear no relationship to what she actually does, the theory is therefore concerned with thought, not behaviour.

## 2.  Piaget's Theory of Moral Development.
Piaget was concerned with children's judgements between right and wrong. He presented pairs of stories to children, both stories containing acts which could be defined as naughty; in one a child had deliberately committed a naughty

act which resulted in a minor outcome, and in the other the child had acted with a good motive but the act had resulted in a major outcome, e.g. a small hole cut purposely in a dress or a big hole cut accidentally while trying to be helpful by cutting out the dress.

Piaget identified two levels of moral reasoning.

(i)    Children under 9 years approx.
       **Moral realism or heteronomous level.** Children think that all rules are 'God given' and should be obeyed. A child at this stage judges the morality of an act in terms of consequences and does not consider the intentions behind the act.

(ii)   Children over 9 years approx.
       **Moral relativism or autonomous level.** Children realize that rules are created by people and that rules can change as the need arises; they realize that morality can depend on intentions as well as consequences.

3.    **Freud's Theory of Moral Development.**
During the oedipus/electra complex the superego develops which through the childs identification with the same-sex parent is the child's internalization of the parents values, beliefs, etc. and which acts as a conscience. Part of the super-ego is the ego ideal, the child's ideas about behaviour her parents would approve. This develops through rewards for such behaviours. Moral anxiety may arise if these internalized ideas and rules are abused and broken.

**Criticisms of Freud:** (See Freud's Psychoanalytic Theory).


# DEVELOPMENT OF AGGRESSION

**Theories of the development of aggression.** Such theorists as Freud and Lorenz view aggression as being inherent (innate) in human beings, while others, such as Skinner, view aggression as learnt behaviour.

1.    **The Sears Study. (Sears Macoby & Levin 1957).**
The researchers conducted a large scale study of child-rearing patterns. They interviewed several hundred mothers and performed correlations between stated child rearing practices and stated resulting behaviours.

They found that parents differed widely in their approach to controlling hostile acts, although almost all of them recognized the importance of control. They

found some mothers who did not permit any aggr
more permissive. They postulated a relationship bet
the child's level of aggression.

**Parents**

| Highly Permissive | Highly agg get their ov aggressive t ...our is reinforced. |
|---|---|
| Physically Punish Aggression | Aggressive children - punishment increased child's frustration and led to more aggression. |
| Restrictive but not very punitive | Least aggressive. |

Further analysis showed that children were more likely to be aggressive when parents displayed - high anxiety about child rearing, low self esteem, mother had low esteem for father, and dissatisfaction with situation.

## 2. John & Elizabeth Newson's (1968) Study in Nottingham.

They investigated how much parents encouraged children to be aggressive. They conducted an interview study of 700 families with four year old children. 61% of the mothers reported that they had on at least one accasion told their children to hit back at other children when attacked. Most mothers however did set limits on what was allowable. i.e. encouragement by parents may further the development of aggression.

## 3. Bandura (1963) and Bandura, Ross & Ross (1961 - 1963)

Children imitate aggressive behaviour displayed by models (see Social Learning Theory). Bandura, Ross and Ross 1961 proposed that parental behaviour causes a child's aggression. They interviewed the parents of hyper-aggressive boys and found that parental rejection and punishment occured before the child showed aggressive tendencies. (See also Bandura & Walters 1959).

## 4. Freudian View of Aggression.

This proposes that when children have aggressive feelings towards parents, a conflict is created because the child loves the parent and fears that the loved one may become angry. The child's anger is therefore repressed or displaced, i.e. the feelings of anger are prevented from entering awareness or the feelings are focused on some other object.

**in Aggression.**

accounts, including those of other cultures, indicate a higher degree
sive behaviour among males than females (See Macoby 1966, Macoby
klin 1974).

However amounts of aggression do differ across societies and in the majority
of cultures parents tolerate or encourage greater aggression among sons than
daughters. Therefore although the effect may be genetic it may also be highly
influenced by environmental factors.

**Studies of Aggression across Cultures.** Sampson (1971) states that the childhood
of the Iatmul head hunters of New Guinea was characterized by humiliation
and pain. Ritualized agression was an integral part of the culture. As adults
the more human scalps they acquired the more important they became. Mead
(1937) found that in the Arapesh tribe in New Guinea males and female's were
brought up in a non-aggressive manner and in adulthood were gentle and co-
operative.

This indicates that there are strong environmental influences e.g. available
models, norms, reinforcement of behaviour which influence the development
of aggression.

## SEX ROLES

1.  **Biological Aspects of Sex Roles.**

Physical sexual characteristics are determined by the chromosonal
arrangement of one of the twenty three pairs of chromosomes. The females
pair contain two X chromosomes and the male's contain an X and a Y
chromosome. Girl XX Boy XY. There is a critical prenatal period for sexual
differentiation (Money 1977). By the first six weeks after conception every
embryo possesses a pair of undifferentiated glands which may become either
testes or ovaries and two sets of tissues which are the starting point of male
and female sex organs. At some point during the seventh or eigth week the sex
chromosomes exert a brief control which results in the glands of genetic males
developing into testes and those of genetic females into ovaries.

After birth the sex organs continue to mature and other things such as the
proportion of muscle tissue and fat also differentiate boys from girls. At puberty
the child attains sexual maturity.

The events of conception, during the foetal period and at puberty constitute
the principal biological contributions to a person's sex.

2.  **Social and cultural aspects of the development of gender roles.**

A person's 'sex' is biologically determined; a person's gender however, their
feelings with respect to masculinity and femininity, are psychologically

determined. Although sex and gender are the same for most people, this is not necessarily true for everyone. Sex-roles and sex-role identity are learnt, and studies suggest that many of the differences between males and females are due to socialization and cultural factors.

**Sex-role stereotypes** — rigid fixed ideas of what is appropriate masculine and feminine behaviour, they are present in nearly every culture. Children are put under strong pressure to conform to these sex-role stereotypes.

The learning of sex-roles begins in infancy and caretakers often respond differently to boys and girls even at six months of age. Some factors which influence the learning and development of sex-roles are

(a) **Reinforcement**

Fagot (1978) demonstrates that parents consistently react more favourably (i.e. reinforce the behaviour) when children engage in behaviour appropriate to their sex and react negatively when their children engage in behaviour inappropriate to their sex.

(b) **Imitation.**

Children learn through imitation of a same sex model, usually the same sex parent in early years. Commercial toys reinforce the sex roles that children are expected to imitate e.g. dolls etc. for girls, cars and trains for boys.

(c) **Identification.**

Children unconsciously identify with the same-sex model which they choose to imitate.

Freud's view of sex-role identification is proposed in his phallic stage when children are experiencing either the oedipus or electra complexes. (See Freuds Psychoanalytic Theory).

The physical changes that occur at adolescence increase the pressure for sex-role appropriate behaviour and society in terms of the media, social groups, and businesses reinforce sexual stereotypes.

3. **Cultural Factors.**

Mead (1935) after studying three different societies in New Guinea felt that culture had a strong influence on sex-roles and sex differences. The three tribes she studied were

(a) **The Arapesh**
Both men and women were trained to be co-operative, unagressive and responsive to the needs and demands of others. Males and females were equally nurturant.

(b) **The Mundugumor**
Both sexes were equally aggressive and competitive and both developed as ruthless individuals with the maternal, cherishing aspects of personality at a minimum.

(c) **The Tchambuli**
Each sex behaved differently from the other, but their sex-roles were the opposite of those in western culture. Women were dominant, impersonal and the managing partner and men were less responsible and emotionally dependent. Men spent time shopping and trading and paying attention to their physical appearance, whereas women were assertive, business-like and supported the family.

Other aspects of child-rearing practices and infant-parent interaction. Child rearing practices can also have an effect on the socialization of the child in the following areas.

(i) Conscience
(ii) Independence
(iii) Achievement Motivation.

## THE DEVELOPMENT OF THE SELF CONCEPT.

The self concept is made up of two elements.

1. **The Self Image.** This is how a person describes herself. e.g. I am a girl, I am a student, I am tall.
    It is the descriptive part of the self concept.

2. **Self-esteem.** This is how favourably a person regards herself. e.g. I am interesting, I am popular.
    Self esteem is the evaluative part of the self concept.

Generally people are constantly being put into categories by other people and people learn which categories they are put in, eventually seeing themselves as fitting into these categories. This contributes towards the formation of the self image.

People are also categorized as more or less rewarding or powerful or interesting; again they learn how they are categorized and this contributes towards the formation of the self-esteem.

Michael Argyle (1969) proposes that a self image can only be sustained if other people accept it and react accordingly; e.g. a person could not maintain an image of himself as the king of France for very long if nobody reacted to him as the king of France. Argyle also proposes that there is an element of self-presentation in behaviour in that people act in certain ways to try and get others to classify them in the way they want to be classified.

The way the self image and self-esteem develop are probably influenced by several factors.

## 1.    The Reactions of Others.

Cooley, (1902) proposed that people look at the reactions of others to find out what they themselves are like. Children are often being told by adults how clever, tall, beautiful they are and this contributes towards the formation of the self-image and the self-esteem. If people react towards a person in such a way that implies she is boring e.g. eyes wander when she talks to them, they yawn, then that person if she is sensitive to this will begin to see herself as boring, i.e. her self image and self-esteem will be affected.

Guthrie (1938) describes how changes in self image lead to a change in behaviour and become self-reinforcing. A group of male students played a joke on a dull female student - they decided to treat her as though she was attractive, interesting and popular and by the end of the year she came to think of herself as interesting and popular and her behaviour and self-confidence had changed.

## 2.    Comparison with others.

If a person who was five feet tall lived in a land where all the people were only three feet six inches tall then that person would regard himself as being tall. If the same person lived in a land where everybody was six feet tall then that person would regard himself as being small. We form our self image and self esteem by comparing ourselves with others. However people are usually realistic in making comparisons and compare themselves with people who are similar to them. For example a girl who plays tennis for the local club team does not decide how good she is by comparing herself with a professional player but by comparing herself with others in the team.

Rosenberg 1965 found that adolescents had greater self-esteem if comparatively they did well at school and were of higher social class.

3.  **The effect of roles played**

The role a person plays e.g. student, results in a corresponding self-image. Merton (1957) found that as they progress through their training medical students gradually begin to see themselves as doctors.

This is also influenced by the reaction of others as patients begin to react to them as doctors.

4.  **Identification with Models.**

When a person identifies with a model she feels to some extent that she posseses some of the model's qualities and this will influence self-image and self-esteem.

**Body Image.**

How a person views his or her body contributes towards the formation of self-image and self-esteem. At puberty, the beginning of adolescence, the size and shape of the body begin to change. Adolescents become extremely sensitive and perceptive about their body size and shape and the mass media influence this with stereotyped images of beautiful people. One condition which occurs in adolescence is anorexia nervosa - the dieting disease, where young girls subject themselves to intense dieting either to counteract overweight or to achieve idealized body proportions. Dwyer and Mayer (1968-69) found that there are many perfectly normal adolescents who are medically healthy but who consider themselves obese and wish to lose weight.

Hamachek (1973) has found that late maturing boys have a more diffiuclt adjustment than early maturers because they tend to be behind in growth, weight and strength which affects performance in athletics and the late maturer is generally treated as a younger, more immature individual. Thus he may continue to act in an immature way, being rebellious and aggressive, therefore his self-image is affected by the reaction of others.

# 4

# SOCIAL INTERACTION

## METHODS IN SOCIAL PSYCHOLOGY

Social psychology considers relationships between social institutions, social groups and individual behaviour, within the larger social influence of a culture.

In order to understand this social behaviour, social psychologists use different methods of investigation.

### 1.    Experiments in the Laboratory

The independent variable is manipulated and changes in the dependent variable are measured while it is attempted to keep all other extraneous variables, which may have unwanted effects on the experiment under control.

**Advantages.** The researcher can control the experimental situation very closely and carefully, therefore attempting to avoid any unwanted or uncontrolled effects.

**Disadvantages.** A laboratory is an unreal situation and therefore subjects may behave differently in the laboratory than they would in a similar real life situation, for several reasons:-

(a)    because the situation is unnatural
(b)    because they feel that the experimenter is an important and responsible person and they should behave in the way they think she wants them to.

Another disadvantage of much reported social psychology laboratory research is that much of the American research has been carried out using only college students as subjects. This makes if difficult to **generalize** the results of such experiments to the population as a whole, as it has been proposed that the results are therefore only applicable to college students.

### 2.    Field Experiments.

This is the type of experiment which is conducted in the natural setting.

**Advantages** - Increases the ability to generalize the results to the real world.

**Disadvantages** - There is a loss of control of the relevant variables.

**General advantage of experiments** - can test cause and effect relationships between variables.

**General disadvantages of experiments.**
(a)  The experimenter is both ethically and legally responsible for what happens to subjects and sometimes experiments may have unpredicted effects on subjects, for example, may cause depression, shame or even a heart attack.

(b)  The knowledge that a subject may have that she is participating in an experiment may affect her behaviour.

(c)  Situations created in the laboratory may be so different from the real world that generalizability of results to a larger population is not possible.

**Survey Research**
In survey research information (known as data) is collected from a **sample** of people who are said to be **representative** of the larger **population.**

**Methods employed in survey research.**

1.  **Interview studies.** This involves interviewers asking a sample of people questions and recording their answers.

2.  **Questionnaire studies.** Questionnaires on topics are designed and delivered to a selected sample of people who then fill them in.

**Advantages.**
(a)  Survey research can ask people to reveal behaviour and feelings which have been experienced in real situations.

(b)  If samples of people are selected at random it is possible to generalize the results to a larger population.

(c)  Questionnaire surveys especially can be carried out relatively cheaply.

**Disadvantages.**

(a) Respondents may not answer questions truthfully either because they cannot remember or because they wish to present themselves in a socially acceptable manner.

(b) It is difficult to establish cause and effect relationships from survey data as other variables which could have had an effect may not have been considered in the questionnaire or interview.

(c) It may be difficult to obtain a random sample of the population because some people who are selected refuse to answer questions or it may be difficult to obtain a full list of the population from which to select a random sample.

## Observational Methods

When using observational methods the researcher watches what is going on and records what is observed using a variety of different techniques.

## Non-Participant Observation

The researcher observes and records behaviour which she makes no attempt to control. The researcher may use a system which allows her to record behaviours in categories such as the Bales Interaction Analysis Matrix used for observation of behaviour in groups. The subjects are observed in their natural setting.

## Advantages

(a) It is possible to gather information about situations in which it would be unethical or impractical to perform experiments for example, the effects on children of transfer from infant to junior schools.

(b) Some researchers feel that behaviour will only occur in its true form in free, natural situations. Ethologists, e.g. Lorenz, frequently used this method.

## Disadvantages

(a) Observers may be biased and record their own interpretation of what they are observing. If observers use predetermined schedules of observation they may feel that they should fit all behaviour into one or another category, even though there may not be a suitable category for it on the schedule.

(b) If people are aware that they are being observed they may not behave naturally.

(c) It is not possible to imply cause and effect relationships from observation studies, because unobserved factors of which the observer is unaware may have an influence.

**Participant Observation.**

The observer becomes a participant in what she is observing. It can range from complete participation by the observer where nobody knows that she is observing, to fairly limited participation with people aware of what she is doing e.g. Whyte (1955) study in Boston of an Italian slum gang.

**Advantages.** The observer is able to experience and therefore gain insight into the behaviour she is studying. It enables the researcher to gain a greater understanding than other methods.

**Disadvantages.**
(a) It is difficult while participating to keep a record of what is happening.

(b) It is not possible to imply cause and effect relationships.

(c) If the observer becomes involved in the situation it is difficult for her to view objectively what is happening. Therefore observer bias may affect the observations.


## NON-VERBAL COMMUNICATION.

The types of things people say are obviously important in forming an impression of that person. Recent research suggests that non-verbal information is also very important particularly in managing the immediate social situation and supporting verbal communication.

**Examples of non-verbal communication.**

| | |
|---|---|
| Posture | Eye contact |
| Facial Expressions | Physical appearance |
| Gestures | Orientation |
| Touch | Non-verbal aspects |
| Proximity | of speech. |

## Functions of Non-verbal signals (Argyle 1969)

**Showing attention and responding.** When two people engage in conversation there must be continuous evidence that each is attending and responding to the other. People usually start conversations by taking up positions so that they are sufficiently close together and by making eye contact. Continuous evidence during the encounter that the other is attending and responding is provided by eye-movements, head nods and gestures. The conversation is usually ended by withdrawal of these cues and changes in position or orientation.

**Controlling channels of communication.** Interactors have to take it in turns to speak and listen, and speech itself cannot be used to decide who shall speak or for how long. head nods and eye movements are often used to control communication channels but often people do not seem to be aware of making or receiving these signals.

**Interpersonal Attitudes.** Argyle argues that attitudes such as
> friendly - hostile
> inferior - superior
> sexual attraction

are mainly signalled non-verbally by means of facial and postural cues.

**Self Presentation.** Clothes, tone of voice, way of standing etc. all give an impression about how a person sees him/herself.

**Emotional states.** Information on emotional states is conveyed by facial expressions and tone of voice.

**Intimacy.** Argyle proposes that non-verbal signals are used to establish intimacy

$$\text{Intimacy} = f \left[ \begin{array}{l} \text{proximity} \\ \text{eye contact} \\ \text{smiling} \\ \text{personal topics of conversation} \end{array} \right.$$

If one of these variables is manipulated, one or more of the others should move in a direction to compensate for the change in level of intimacy.

**Illustrations.** Speech is often accompanied by gestures which accompany and illustrate what is being said.

**Feedback.** Information on how the verbal information is being received is collected by clues from the listener's face, e.g. raised eyebrows or movements of the mouth. Communication of this type may be partly involuntary but in most cultures people are aware of, and control, their facial expressions. Evidence of interest is also provided by the appropriate proximity and orientation.

# CONFORMITY

**Definitions:**
(a)   Yielding to group expectations.

(b)   A change in belief or behaviour due to real or imagined group pressure.

Conformity implies some degree of conflict between what the group demands of the individual and what the individual would otherwise do.

The central question when considering conformity is what happens when the individuals privately held attitudes, perceptions and definitions of the situation conflict with the position taken by the group.

Several studies are given as examples below which demonstrate what happens when the individual's privately held attitudes, perceptions, and definitions of the situation conflict with the position taken by the group.

**Muzafer Sherif 1935.**

The autokinetic effect was employed in this study. The autokinetic effect is the phenomenon that occurs when a pinpoint of light is viewed in what is otherwise a totally dark room: a totally stationary light will appear to move.

In one experiment he brought a group of subjects into a dark room to observe a pinpoint of light and then asked them to estimate how far the light moved. After a series of trials Sherif observed that the range of estimates by the subjects began to converge toward the mean.

**Criticism.** This experiment is equally concerned with consensus as there is no figure acting as a model with whom subjects conform.

**Solomon Asch 1951, 1952, 1956.**

A group of seven to nine subjects were assembled in a classroom supposedly to take part in an experiment on visual judgement. The subjects were first shown a white card with a single black line. From a second card with three lines the subjects were asked to choose the line which was the same length as the line on the first card. The subjects announced their answers one at a time, in the order in which they were seated. However, only the last individual in the sequence was a subject; the others were in league with the experimenter and responded according to a prearranged plan, i.e. stooges. During the first two trials, each of the stooges were instructed to give the correct response. Following this, they began systematically to give a preselected incorrrect response.

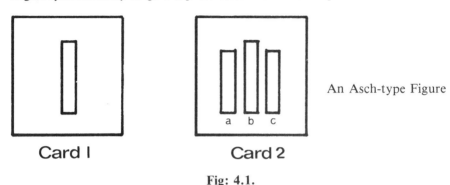

Card 1          Card 2

An Asch-type Figure

**Fig: 4.1.**

**Results.** Under ordinary circumstances when tested alone individuals made mistakes less than 1% of the time.

Under group pressure the subjects accepted the wrong judgements in 36·8% of the cases. However, individuals differed markedly in their responses, some subjects were completely independent, never agreeing with the group on test trials, whereas other subejcts conformed almost all the time.

**Variations.**
**What size majority?** In one series of studies the size of the opposition was varied from one to fifteen persons. The effectiveness of the group pressure increased markedly up to a group size of three, but further increases added little to the overall effect.

**Does the group decision have to be unanimous?** If the subject had a supporting partner then conformity disappeared. Even when one of the stooges was instructed to disagree with both the group and the subject, the rate of conformity was reduced.

**Criticisms.** The experiment may not be like real life in that subjects were expected to instantly voice an opinion, whereas in real life people withhold comments or opinions if they are not sure.

The subjects may not have been conforming to the group, but may have conformed because they thought that that was what the experimenter expected of them.

**Richard Crutchfield 1954.** Crutchfield tested five subjects at once. Each was seated in a cubicle containing an electric panel. Each subject had to respond to a series of questions projected onto the wall in front of her. Each was told she was the last to answer and the answers of the other subjects would be shown by lights on the panel. The lights on the panel were actually controlled by the experimenter and on each trial all five subjects saw the same display of lights.

Subjects were asked, for example, which is the larger, the star or the circle.

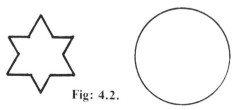

**Fig: 4.2.**

**Results.** 23 out of 50 subjects, 46% of subjects, conformed to say the star was larger.

Military subjects were also tested to see if they would agree with the statement "I doubt whether I would make a good leader" and other similar statements.

**Results.** When tested alone no subject agreed with the statement.

When tested in the conformity situation in the cubicles 37% did agree.

## OBEDIENCE

Obedience basically is following orders, even when such orders might cause other people pain, danger and perhaps even death.

**The Milgram Experiments. (1963, 1964, 1965, 1974).**

The basic experiment at Yale University was that two people came to the laboratory to take part in a study of memory and learning. One of them designated a 'teacher' and the other a 'learner'. The experimenter explains that the study is concerned with the effects of punishment on learning. The learner is conducted into a room, seated in a chair, her arms strapped to prevent excessive movement and an electrode attached to her wrist. She is told that she is to learn a list of word pairs, whenever she makes an error, she will receive electric shocks of increasing intensity.

However the real focus of the experiment is the 'teacher'. After watching the learner being strapped into place, she is taken into the main experimental room seated before an impressive shock generator. It's main feature is a line of 30 switches ranging from 15 volts to 450 volts in 15 volt increments. There are also verbal signs which range from 'SLIGHT SHOCK' to 'DANGER SEVERE SHOCK'. The teacher is told that she is to administer the learning test to the person in the other room. When the learner responds correctly, the teacher moves on to the next item, when she gives an incorrect answer, the teacher is to give her an electric shock. She is to start at 15 volts and to increase the level each time the woman makes an error.

The 'teacher' is a genuinely naive subject who has come to the laboratory to participate in an experiment. The 'learner' or victim is an actor who actually receives no shock at all.

During the experiment, for the 'teacher' (subject) there is intense conflict. On the one hand, the obvious suffering of the victim presses her to stop, but on the other, the experimenter, a legitimate authority to whom the subject feels some commitment encourages her to continue. Each time the subject hesitates to administer shock the experimenter orders her to continue. To extricate herself from the situation the subject must make a clear break with authority.

**Results.**(1)  62·5% of the subjects went as far as 450 volts. (2)   All subjects who began giving shocks continued at least to 300 volts.

**Variations.**
1.   Experiment conducted in a sleazy office building rather than the plush official surroundings of the university.
     **Result.** 50% of subjects obeyed.
2.   Victim in the same room as the subject and could be seen by her.
     **Result.** 40% of subjects obeyed.
3.   Subject required to hold the 'learners' arm down on the electrodes.
     **Result.** 30% of subjects obeyed.
4.   The experimenter in a white laboratory coat left the room and issued instructions to the subject by telephone.
     **Result.** The obedience level dropped almost to zero.

**Conclusions.** Milgram believed that the major factor was the presence of the experimenter in a white laboratory coat. Subjects obeyed because they were obeying a man in authority, in a white coat who knew what he was doing.

A lesser factor was the nearness of the learner.

**Three different types of conformity.**
**Kelman 1961**
1.   **Compliance.** Going along with the group demands because noncompliance could result in punishment or loss of reward.

2.  **Identification.** The individual goes along with another or adopts an idea not because it is intrinsically satisfying but because he or she desires to be like the influencer.

3.  **Internalization.** The individual chooses a particular action not because of the threat of punishment for not doing so and not because another with whom she or he identifies urges that particular course of action, but because he or she really believes that it is the correct and appropriate way things should be done.

## WORK

Views in the western world of the underlying motives that people have for working have changed with increasing prosperity and with changes in ideas of the nature of humankind.*

### Frederick Taylor 1920's Rational Economic Man.

People were seen as rational, and motivated largely by self-interest and money. Human performance was regarded as if it had a machine-like nature. Frederick Taylor proposed that people, like machines, could be managed scientifically and treated in a standardised fashion. Money incentives were what was needed to keep people working. This concept of human nature directed research towards the physical and psychological aspects of work performance, such as the effects of noise, light, temperature and fatigue on human responses.

### The Hawthorne Studies (1930's) Social - Man.
### Roethlisberger and Dickson (1939)

These studies conducted in 1927-1932 involved testing the effects of various work conditions such as light intensity, the frequency and length of rest periods and the type of supervision on work performance. Female employees were selected for the studies and were placed in a special observation room. For two years, the lighting, rest periods and supervision were varied and it appeared that each change caused production to increase. The most popular explanation of the results was that the physical changes were in fact irrelevant to the productivity of the group. What seemed to play a more important part was the fact that the girls had been given attention by the researchers and made to feel important.

**Criticisms.**

1.  Recent statistical reinterpretation of the Hawthorne data suggests that the experimental variables, light, rest periods etc, did account for most of the variability inquantity and quality of output (Franke and Kaul 1978).

2.  Individual differences are disregarded. Some people do enjoy working alone and some are primarily interested in financial rewards.

**Maslow & Herzberg 1950's Self-Actualizing Man.**
Other researchers such as Herzberg, McClelland and Maslow have drawn attention to the fact that work may involve other needs apart from those economic and social needs, such as the desire for achievement and recognition, and the need to carry out interesting work.

**Abraham Maslow 1954.**
Maslow linked together biological, social and personal needs into a hierarchy
5.  Self actualization — (self fulfilment)
4.  Self esteem — (self respect)
3.  Social — (acceptance by others)
2.  Safety — (need for threat free environment)
1.  Physiological — (food, drink etc.)

he suggests that there is an order of priority in these needs. Lower needs (physiological, safety, etc.) must be satisfied before people become interested in the higher needs.

**Criticism.** The order of needs may reflect priorities in American society only.

**Herzberg's Two Factor Theory. 1957.**
This theory is similar to Maslow's in stressing a hierarchy of human motivation. Interviews were carried out in which people were asked to describe times when they were very satisfied and very dissatisfied at work Herzberg found that two different groups of activities were involved.

Dissatisfaction at work was associated with what he calls
**Hygiene factors**
poor company policy
supervision
security
working conditions
interpersonal relations.

Satisfaction was associated with
**Motivating Factors**
  achievement
  advancement
  recognition
  responsibility
  type of work.
Salary caused both good and bad experiences.

Absence of 'hygiene factors' produces dissatisfaction, presence does not give satisfaction, though improvement in 'hygiene' may give short term motivation.

'Motivating factors' are the only source of long term satisfaction at work.

**Criticism.** Possibly the way in which the research of Herzberg was carried out affected the kind of replies he got. If evidence about motivation is collected using different techniques Herzberg's two factors do not appear and this suggests that his basic idea is wrong.

**Douglas McGregor 1960**
**Theory X and Theory Y**
  McGregor proposes that the ideas behind the earlier theories, such as that of Taylor, are that:-

— all workers dislike work and will avoid it if they can.

— most people have to be coerced, directed and threatened to get them to make adequate effort at work.

— most people prefer to be directed, wish to avoid responsibility and have relatively little ambition.

These ideas about people he calls Theory X.

He proposes an alternative theory based on different assumptions about human personality and job satisfaction:-

— people want to contribute to creative solutions,

— people will, under the right conditions, positively seek responsibility,

— the average human being does not naturally dislike work. Depending on comfortable conditions work may be a source of satisfaction.

These ideas about people he calls Theory Y.

**General Criticism.**
  None of the above theories take individual differences into account. For example, some people do enjoy working alone and some are primarily interested in financial rewards. Differences in past experience, educational background, age and social class, will all affect a worker's perception of her job and the expectations she has of it.

Different people are probably motivated by many different factors.

**Working in Groups.**

The importance of working in groups for productivity was first suggested by the hawthorne studies (Roethlisberger and Dickson 1939) where groups are not organized formally at work, unofficial groupings appear.

Working in groups has a number of advantages.

(a)    Groups can co-operate over large tasks.

(b)    Division of labour can enable group members to use their specialized skills.

(c)    Group members may collaborate to protect their interests against action by management.

(d)    Members of a group can help each other.

# 5

# THE PRACTICAL APPLICATIONS OF PSYCHOLOGICAL RESEARCH

## BEHAVIOUR MODIFICATION

### Classical conditioning techniques.

### 1.   Systematic Desensitization.

In 1920 J.B. Watson and R. Rayner demonstrated the classical conditioning of fear using a nine-month old infant named Albert. Albert was shown a white rat which initially aroused only the boy's curiosity. Then the rat was presented to the boy at the same time as a gong was banged close by, making a loud alarming sound, which caused Albert to cry. After about five such pairings, the sight of the rat alone caused Albert to cry. This clearly demonstrates that fear can be learned and also, since Albert became frightened of objects that resembled a white rat such as other white furry animals and even balls of cotton-wool, that the fear showed the features of any conditioned response. Watson and Rayner proposed that the fear could be eliminated by using the principle of reciprocal inhibition in a step-by-step procedure. Reciprocal inhibition is the mutual antagonism of two competing responses such as eating and fear. It is impossible to be very frightened and eat at the same time, if you try to do both either you will overcome the fear and eat or you will lose your appetite and be frightened. Watson and Rayner suggested inhibiting the fear response in Albert by giving him sweets to eat. With the fear response under control they would then present Albert with a caged rat in the doorway of the room and step-by-step bring the animal nearer and finally out of the cage. The fear response would then be extinguished.

In the 1950's J. Wolpe developed and formalised this procedure which is now known as Systematic Desensitization. Instead of feeding their patients, psychologists use relaxation to inhibit the fear response in order to help people overcome irrational fears called **phobias.** Eg. arachnophobia - fear of spiders - would be treated by teaching the patient to relax, then asking them to imagine fearful situations involving spiders, eventually bringing real spiders closer and closer to the patient. For phobias with a specific stimulus which causes the fear, systematic desensitization is very successful.

## 2. Aversion Therapy.

This is simply the implementation of the basic classical conditioning procedure in an attempt to train patients to associate an unpleasant event with some behaviour which they wish to give up. A good example is the treatment of alcoholism. An emetic (a substance which causes vomiting) is paired with alcohol repeatedly until alcohol alone causes the vomiting reflex:-

Alcohol (CS) + Emetic (UCS) ──────→'Nausea and vomiting (UCR)'
Alcohol (CS)─────────────────────→ 'Nausea and vomiting (CR)'

Unfortunately aversion therapy has a high relapse rate, in other words the improvement due to aversion therapy is often only temporary and patients revert to old drinking habits.

## Operant conditioning techniques.
### 1. Token Economy Systems.

A token economy system is a formalised regime of secondary reinforcement (usually plastic tokens, hence the name) for any behaviour which those operating the regime so desire. Such schemes have been used to increase behaviour related to self sufficiency, personal hygiene and tidyness and non-violent social interaction in psychiatric and subnormal hospitals. Each patient on the ward is rewarded with a token for various behaviors such as dressing and undressing unaided, washing unaided etc. The tokens can be exchanged at the end of each week for primary reinforcers such as tobacco, sweets etc. It is important that each patient has an individually tailored program within the regime as a whole, so that each patient can earn a similar number of rewards. If the system gets out of balance, some patients may not be reinforced and experience the system as punishing.

A well run token economy can produce dramatic improvements in behaviour, but is very costly in terms of staff, since the nurses need to be vigilant in order to administer the reinforcements quickly and fairly.

Most of us have experienced low-key token economies at school. Perhaps you recognise a token economy system disguised as house-point system in your primary or secondary school? Such systems if well run can powerfully shape social behaviour of young people.

### 2. Behaviour Shaping.

Isaacs, Thomas and Goldiamond (1960) reported the case of a catatonic schizophrenic whose behaviour was shaped over a period of weeks. The patient had been silent and immobile for many years, and by accident it was discovered that he was interested by a chewing gum packet. This was exploited and used by the psychologist as a reinforcer to increase gradually the number of eye movements, lip movements and eventually meaningful vocalizations made by the patient.

More recently a similar method has been used in an attempt to train autistic children to speak. A shaping procedure is used, based on speech therapy exercises with food as a reinforcer. Unfortunately the relapse rate with autistic children is very high, with very few children able to string words together in phrases or sentences even after many months of training.

**Discussion of Behaviour Modification.**

Some critics of these methods believe that behavior therapy treats the **symptoms** only and the real cause is left untreated. There is some evidence that after apparently successful treatment with behaviour therapy, other symptoms emerge after a short delay. This is known as symptom substitution. However, the issue is essentially a philosophical and theoretical one - behaviourists believe that there is **only** behaviour (symptoms) and that our search for deep causes is futile. Some behavioral treatments are spectacularly successful and others dismal in their success rates. This may be because the successful ones such as systematic desensitization and token economies are re-training methods aimed at behaviour which was faultily learned in the first place, such as an irrational fear or poor personal hygiene.

The methods showing little success are often trying to modify behaviour which is probably not the result of faulty learning. Childhood autism is not an example of faulty learning on the child's part, and alcoholism usually reflects personal problems in other areas of the patients life.


## BIOFEEDBACK

In 1969 N.E. Miller and L.W. DiCara showed that instrumental conditioning could be used to change involuntary behaviour such as autonomic nervous system reflexes. Previously it had been assumed that instrumental conditioning could only affect voluntary behaviour and that classical conditioning alone could affect reflexive behaviour. Miller and DiCara taught rats to raise and lower their heart-rate and blood-pressure for reward. In order to make sure that the rats were not activating a reflex by contracting or relaxing their muscles, Miller and DiCara paralysed them with a curare-like drug. This meant that food could not be used as a reward, so the rats received a small electric current from an electrode implanted in the hypothalamus. There are many sites in the hypothalamus and surrounding area which when stimulated act as reinforcers. Such sites are sometimes misleadingly called 'pleasure centres'.

This work has stimulated a number of medical uses called **biofeedback techniques** in which human patients are trained to lower their blood pressure, lower their heart rate or dilate blood vessels for reward. For humans, though, the rewards are simply encouragement from nursing staff or the sense of achievement of having succeeded. The important factor in the technique is **feedback** of physiological change to the patient - hence the name.

## THE FAMILY, HOME AND SURROGATES

1.  **Parenting.**
Parental behaviour affects children in many ways. Perhaps the most important are that (a) they act as models for children, (b) they have expectations which they transmit to their children about the ways in which they want them to behave, (c) they control the rewards and discipline their children receive. (see Social and emotional development). Separation from parents can also have an effect on children (see deprivation studies).

2.  **Adoption and Fostering.**
Bowlby (1951), Goldfarb (1945) and Spitz (1949) proposed that children brought up in institutions were intellectually retarded, had difficulties in language development and developed a lasting inability to form deep emotional relationships. These abnormalities were thought to be irreversible and were thought to be due to the absence of a warm, continuous relationship with a mother figure during the critical years of early childhood. Rutter (1972) proposed that as institutions improve, abnormalities in development appear less marked. Clarke (1976) proposes that the concepts of critical periods, irreversible effects and affection bonds, used to explain institutional deprivation are now less widely accepted.

**Tizzard and Rees (1974)** studied 65 children reared from infancy in three residential nurseries. The staff changed often but there was a high staff-child ratio. There was official disapproval of close personal relationships between the children and the staff. However there was very good material provision for the children, they had lots of books, toys and outings. Between 2 years and 4½ years, 24 were adopted and 15 restored to their mothers. At the age of 4½ the IQ's of all the children were at least average, but the adopted children had higher IQ's and appeared more stable than those remaining in an institution or restored to their mothers. The adopted children were also friendlier, more talkative and more co-operative than the institutional children. However the adopted children were more attention seeking and overfriendly than a similar group of home-reared children (control group).

In December 1975 when they were about eight years of age all the children were traced, and it was found, of those who had not moved away or whose families did not refuse to see the researchers, that their IQ's had not changed very much from what they were at 4½ years. However some of the adopted children had grown difficult to manage and were still over-affectionate. They tended to be restless, fidgety and quarrelsome and had problems in forming friendships with other children.

**The Adoption of older children.** Kadushin (1970) studied 91 families who adopted children who had been removed from their natural families becuase of neglect or abuse. The average age of adoption in the study was 7·2 years and the children were researched again at approximately 14 years of age (longitudinal study). The results stated that the children showed a greater degree of psychological health and stability than might have been expected given their bad experiences in childhood. Their abilities to form interpersonal relationships were considered fairly good, but the older the child was at the time of adoption the less good was the formation of relationships.

**Meier (1962)** Completed a follow up study of 61 adults who had grown up in foster care. About half the group had been removed from home before 5 years of age and all of them had spent at least five years in foster care. When they were discharged from foster care at 18 years they had experienced an average of 5·6 homes. Meier found that most of them as adults were coping well and were well-adjusted individuals.

(See also studies by Tinker 1952, Weller 1965, Rathburn 1964, Roe 1972 and Moss 1963)

Kadushin (1970) argues that children vary in their capacity to deal with potentially traumatic conditions and a healthier environment may help them to survive the damaging influences of earlier abuse.

## Pre-School Provision
**Childminders.** Many mothers wish or find it necessary to work and with insufficient day-nursery places many children are taken to childminders. Childminders are people who take children into their homes and look after them for a few hours or a full day.

The Seebohm committee (1968) proposed that many children under 5 years were being minded in conditions which were dangerous to their health and safety and which would impair their emotional and intellectual development. Mayall and Petrie (1977) in an observation study of 39 childminders in London proposed that children in such situations were sad and passive, their mothers were anxious and harried and the childminders were busy and therefore insensitive to the childrens' needs.

Shinman (1982) carried out a study with two different groups of mothers who were also childminders in priority areas of Inner London. She found that in the majority of cases children's emotional and physical needs were satisfactorily met. However the range of stimulating play materials available was extremely limited.

**Day Nurseries.**

Local authority social services departments usually run day nurseries to cater for children under five 'in special need', e.g. from one parent families. Most of the children attend full-time and most of the staff are qualified nursery nurses.

**Nursery Schools.**

Provided by local education authorites or privately for children between 2 years and 5 years. Normally a morning and afternoon session, 5 days a week and children may attend on a full or part-time basis.

**Playgroups.**

Playgroups are usually run by volunteers and provide an opportunity for children to mix with one another and to play with materials that may not be available in the home. Some playgroups run on a full-time basis operating two sessions a day whereas others only meet for one session (morning or afternoon) a day. Usually playgroups welcome the support and involvement of parents.

## PLAY AND LEARNING

Parry and Archer (1974) propose that the stage for learning is set by the joy and pleasure of play; in playing there are opportunities to explore materials, to construct and create, to discover and destroy. The child also interacts with other children and learns how to mix.

Through play, a child learns how to interact with her environment and her peers, she learns skills and obtains information which enhances her cognitive development.

**Theories of Play.**

1.  **Psychoanalytical theories of Play**

The psychoanalytical approach to play proposes that the dreaming, fantasizing and imagining in play represent the child's effort to deal with the daily problems of life (Freud 1958). Isaacs (1930) sees the dramatic play of children as enabling them to work out their inner conflicts in a safe environment, thus lessening their fears and anxieties, Isaacs (1932) proposes that children do not have to be taught to play or given instructions, they play naturally and through play they learn.

Psychoanalytic theories of play have had a strong influence on nursery practice. Instruction is ruled out, the teacher is there to guide but not to teach.

## 2. Piaget's Theory of Play.

Piaget proposes that the child during play is dominated by her own needs at that moment in time, rather than the demands of the outside world.

### Stages of Play

(a) **Practice or exercise play.** 0 - 18 months the child repeats pleasurable movements and gains mastery over these movements. This stage corresponds to the sensori-motor stage of cognitive development.

(b) **Symbolic Play** 2 years - 7 years. The child has the use of language and creates imaginary situations in which familiar objects can be made to stand for something else in order to fulfil the child's desires of the moment.

(c) **Play with rules.** 7 years onwards. Play ceases to be intuitive and begins to incorporate rules. At first rules are seen as absolute and unchangeable and imposed by some outside authority. Gradually they lose their aura of being absolute, are seen as being flexible and changeable as long as fairness is maintained.

Piaget also used the term **adaption** involving **assimilation and accommodation** in his description of play.

Assimilation is when a child fits something into an already existing schema. For example, when throwing a toy brick, a child is assimilating the brick into the throwing scheme, the brick is turned into something to be thrown.

Accommodation involves the modification of already existing schema to fit incoming information.

For example the child takes in further information about the brick, that it can be used to build with. Piaget proposes that assimilation is what the child is doing when playing in that the child is changing the world to fit with her own understanding.

## 3. Bruner's View of Play.

Bruner (1972) views play as a means of attaining cognitive skills. He sees experimentation of small actions possible during play which can eventually be combined into a well developed skill. Such play allows the child to learn about things such as spatial relations in an informal situation to arrange and rearrange things at will until what she is striving for works, without any pressure of time. This allows the child to develop a flexible use of tools and materials and therefore contribute towards problem solving.

## 4. Corinne Hutt's view of exploration and play.

Hutt (1966) studied preschool children as they encountered a complex object in an experimental playroom. The object was a red rectangular box on four brass legs; on top of the box was a perpendicular stick which could be moved in different directions.

Condition 1 : Moving the stick had no results.

Condition 2 : Moving the stick caused figures to be exposed on one face of the box. (Visual feedback).

Condition 3 : Moving the stick caused a bell and buzzer to sound (auditory feedback)

Condition 4 : Moving the stick caused simultaneous visual and auditory feedback.

Hutt found that at first children actively investigated and experimented with the object in order to discover what it would do. After this exploration phase they began to use the object in game playing while at the same time looking around the room at other toys. The children thus got used to the object and would only investigate it again if they discovered a new property, e.g. visual feedback added. Auditory feedback produced the greatest interest in the toy.

She also observed changes in the children's moods. Initially when experimenting with the toy they were serious and intense. Later they handled the object more casually and were more relaxed. Finally they behaved nonchalantly toward the object, often observing what was going on elsewhere.

Hutt and Bhavrani (1972) revisited the same children five years later. In testing the children, they found that those who had refused to explore the toy were lacking in curiousity and adventure if they were boys, and had difficulties in personality and social adjustment if they were girls. Children who had been active explorers were more likely to score high on tests of creativity and more likely to be judged as curious and independent by their teachers.

Hutt generally proposes that the functions of children's play differ over time and that there is a relationship between exploratory play and the willingness to explore and subsequent personality and cognitive style.

**Play Therapy**

Play therapy is in accord with psychoanalytic views on play in that it endeavours to help children to work out their feelings and anxieties in safe situations. There is less tension and anxiety in play activities than in the 'real' world, so children can use play to explore and learn to cope with their feelings. During play therapy a child may relive painful experiences and may also be able to work out a solution for herself. In 'Dibs In Search of Self', Virginia Axline (1964) the author, describes a child whose father was very strict, demanding and emotionally cold. The child was withdrawn, crawled about the floor and hid under tables. When playing in a sand box he always hid one doll (his father) deep in the sand. However through play sessions he built up a friendly world of dolls for himself in which he could release his anxieties and come to terms with himself through symbolic play.

In play therapy the child is not directed in any way but uses the playroom and playthings in any way she wishes in a safe, non judgemental situation. Toys are provided to enable children to act out feelings or regress to an earlier part of their life.

## Schools.
Most children after the age of 5 years spend the majority of their time each day in school. Knowledge about reading, writing, arithmetic, science, history, technology and the skills associated with these seem to depend on formal education.

## Discovery Learning.
Piaget has proposed that schemata are only developed by active involvement in learning and not by passive absorption of data. Learning by discovery has thus been advocated either where children are left to find things out entirely for themselves or they 'discover' in a partially structured and guided setting.

## Programmed Learning.
Programmed learning originates from the work of Skinner and the principles of instrumental conditioning (see also instrumental conditioning page 21).

The subject matter to be learned is in a carefully arranged progression of information, questions and answers. Each unit of information which appears before a pupil is called a frame. The production of a correct answer by the pupil is reinforcement in that it gives the pupil a sense of satisfaction and it allows a move to the next frame to be made.

A programme which only allows the correct response to be made to the question or information in the frame (stimulus) before the pupil can move onto the next frame (reinforcement) is called a linear programme i.e. the frames are in a straight sequence.

Branching programmes differ from the linear type in that the frames of information are larger and are followed by questions offering several answers of which only one is correct. if the pupil chooses the correct answer she moves onto the next frame; if an incorrect answer is chosen then the pupil has to go on to a remedial frame which will explain why the answer was incorrect repeat the correct information and retest it.

92

| Differences between programmed learning and instrumental conditioning | |
| --- | --- |
| **Programmed Learning** | **Instrumental Conditioning** |
| Many different responses (or answers) are required. Praise or a correct answer may not be reinforcement for some people. | Usually only one response (e.g. pressing a lever) required. Reinforcement is usually in the form of something for which the animal has a basic drive. |

**Advantages of Programmed Learning.**
1. Allows the individual needs of pupils to be met.
2. Gives pupils immediate knowledge of results.
3. Programmes can relieve teachers in order that they can spend more time with individual students.
4. Students can run programmes at their own pace which helps to prevent lack of understanding or boredom.

**Disadvantages of Programmed Learning.**
1. Some teachers feel that programmes prevent pupils from being creative and do not give the opportunity for self expression.
2. Machines and programmes are expensive.
3. Once the novelty has worn off, some pupils may become bored and find the method of learning monotonous.

**Testing in Schools**
**Intelligence Tests**
(See also intelligence tests page 44 )

Interest in defining and measuring intelligence in education arose because it was believed that each individual had a fixed amount of this attribute and that it was possible to measure intelligence and predict people's abilities later in life (This was the basis on which the 11 + was used to allocate children to different schools).

However studies e.g. Bayley (1955) have shown that at age 11 the correlation with IQ at maturity is far from perfect and at younger ages the correlation is so low that the use of intelligence tests for selection purposes becomes highly questionable.

Most intelligence tests aim at assessing such things as reasoning ability, abstract thought, perceptual-motor ability and spatial ability. Scoring involves comparing the number of items answered correctly by a child with the average scores of children of her own age. Using tables and instructions it is also possible to convert the child's score into a mental age which is then divided by her actual age and multiplied by 100 to give an IQ score.

$$IQ = \frac{Mental\ Age}{Chronological\ age} \times 100$$

Nowadays a test is modified in the light of certain statistical techniques which are carried out on the results.

The distribution of scores for each age group is found using representative samples. The mean for the sample is usually converted to 100 and the distribution of scores on each side of the mean is manipulated so that approximately 70% of the scores fall between 85 and 115 (i.e. one standard deviation either side of the mean). For this method to work the distribution of scores has to be **normal or near normal.**

(See data analysis page 101).

A good intelligence test should be **reliable, valid and standardized** (see Methods in Developmental Psychology). A good intelligence test should also be 'culture-fair' — free from cultural biases (not contain questions which people from other countries may not understand or may interpret differently which may unfairly make scores higher or lower).

**Uses of Intelligence Tests.**
1. **Verbal group tests** used to be used as a grammar school selection device. Written instructions and the test are administered to a large group under the same conditions.
2. **Non-verbal group tests.** Used to give addiontal information on such areas as mechanical and spatial skills.
3. **Individual tests.** Used with pre-school, infant school and backward children because writing, reading, concentration and motivation may be a problem, therefore these children cannot be tested in a group situation. The administration of an individual test is highly skilled, the administrator needing to be able to talk to, encourage and extract the best from the children.

Generally intelligence tests are used as predictors of future performance or diagnostic tools. Sometimes they are used to stream children or to spot children who need to attend remedial classes.

**Criticisms of Intelligence Tests.**
1. There is no agreed definition of intelligence and therefore it must be questioned whether intelligence can in fact be measured.
2. Many intelligence tests contain items which assume that a person has received some education. This may not be true and intelligence tests should not measure educational attainment.

3. Intelligence tests are unfair because those who cannot think quickly are penalized.
4. It is possible to give coaching, and for people to learn how to do intelligence tests.
5. Intelligence tests do not accurately predict performance in school, work, employment or other real life situations.

Another method of assessment used in schools is the examination; One of the aims of examinations is to measure attainment. There are several different forms of examinations:
1. Conventional written examinations.
2. Objective type examinations. Information is given in the stem of the question and it is designed so that the answer has to be either recalled from memory or recognized from a collection of possible answers which are given along with the question e.g. multiple choice questions.
3. Practical Examinations e.g. in science subjects.
4. Oral examinations e.g. in languages.
5. Examinations in which part of the final mark is obtained from project work done in school during the year.
The results of examinations are used to diagnose weaknesses and also to predict aptitude for further study or work.

## AGEING AND SENESCENCE

### Methodological problems.
The methods used in the study of ageing are the same as those used in developmental psychology - both areas looking for changes in performance over a period of time. There are three basic methods -
1. **Longitudinal studies.** The performance of a sample of subjects is measured on *at least* two occasions and the differences compared (25 people tested at the ages of 40, 50 and 60).
2. **Cross-sectional studies.** Two or more different but comparable samples of subjects are compared at selected age levels. (We compare the performance of comparable groups of 40, 50 and 60 year-olds)
3. **Cross-longitudinal studies.** Measure the initial performance of different aged groups e.g. 40, 50 and 60 year-olds, and then follow up each group with the same measures over many years.
These different methods often give rise to different results over time for the same variables, so in order to disentangle the various effects, Bromley (1974) suggests using the term **age changes** to describe changes within the same people

due to age and the term **age differences** to indicate the differences between different people (measured at the same time) due to age.

There are many complicating factors to be considered when trying to interpret studies on the effects of age. Imagine two studies, both trying to sort out the effects of age on IQ - firstly a cross-sectional study comparing the IQ's of a group of 40 year-olds with a group of 60 year-olds. We would never be sure whether any differences in IQ were due to the chronological age of the subjects or the **cohort** (the year they were born). The cohort will effect such things as length and type of education, attitudes to education and work, nutrition during childhood etc., all of which might effect IQ throughout life.

So the answer is to conduct a longitudinal study, our second study in this example. Here a group of 40 year-olds were measured in 1960 and again in 1980. Can we make generalisations from our results about the effects of age on IQ in all humans? No. Because we still have a cohort effect. All we can say is that this is how the IQ of people born in 1920 will be affected by age. All the cultural, educational and nutritional variables will change for each cohort.

### Physical effects of ageing

Physiological processes reach a peak around 30 years of age and thereafter gradually decline. The rate of this decline depends upon many factors - heredity, diet, type of work, pollution, health care, socioeconomic class, etc. The various systems and organs of the body show different rates of decline exerting greater or lesser effects on physical, psychological and social abilities.

**Elastic tissue.** There is a gradual loss of elastic fibres in the skin (resulting in sagging and wrinkles). The ear drum loses some of its elasticity, resulting in the loss of hearing of high frequency sounds. The lens of the eye also relies on its elastic properties which decline with age resulting in poor accommodation to short distances.

**Skeleton.** Loss of calcium from the bones results in a greater tendency to fracture. This might also affect the ossicles in the ear and thus affect hearing. Also, a loss of living cells in bone makes the healing of fractures slower in old age, changing a simple break into a serious and complicated disability.

**Brain and nervous system.** From the age of 30 onwards, neurons die at an estimated rate of 30 cells per minute in the C.N.S. This is probably responsible for the loss in brain weight with age of about 20% between the ages of 20 and 80 years old. There seems to be negligible changes in the speed and efficiency of the remaining neurons. It is thought that when brain cell death reaches certain proportions, brain damage may result in **senile dementia,** a distressing collection of physical and psychological symptoms relating to loss of function.

**Endocrine system.** A decrease in gonad function results in the menopause in women and a much slower decline in testicular function in men. Thyroid activity declines, affecting overall metabolism and 'energy'. Insulin production in the pancreas may become erratic, decline or fail completely resulting in diabetes.

The main point regarding physical changes is that the difference between individuals is very great. That is why no ages have been mentioned in the above text. Also the type of health care available is likely to make such changes easier or more uncomfortable to bear. Simply being aware of the physical changes associated with age will help us understand the problems that old people have, and help us prepare for and cope with our own old age, better.

**Psychological effects of ageing.**
**Intelligence.** Here the methodological problems outlined above become complicated by problems of definition. 'Intelligence' is at best an awkward concept to define, but we are helped little if we restrict our discussion to IQ, because the term IQ includes an adjustment for age (see page 94). D. Wechsler worked at devising an adult intelligence test standardised on 2000 men and women aged between 16 and 75 years old. (see standardisation page 29). It is called the Wechsler Adult Intelligence Scale of WAIS. By definition, a person's IQ stays the same over time, but their test performance, both as a child and an adult, may change. No long-term longitudinal studies of age changes in intelligence test performance have been carried out, but the few results available show that over a few years, some people get better with age, some stay the same and some get worse.

Wechsler has produced much evidence from cross-sectional studies of age differences in test performance and has tried to compare the performance of old and young people. He interpreted the results to mean that on certain sub-tests of the WAIS, performance declines with age and on others there is no decline. His views have been heavily criticised however, some workers suggesting that he has underestimated the age differences, and yet others suggesting that he has overestimated!

Until longitudinal data are available, we will not know how age and cohort affect test performance, and even then the conclusions will be arguable!
**Memory.** Although memory changes related to age are highlighted by the WAIS we will deal with them separately.

With an increasing number of psychologists questioning the theoretical aspects of memory, it is inadvisable to use terms like Short Term Memory. But whatever you call it, older people have problems with it when their attention is divided (they have to think about something else at the same time) or they have to do something with the information while holding it (recall the information in reverse order).

If a subject is asked to reproduce a list of numbers eg. 3 9 4 6 2, there are no differences due to age, but if the subject is asked to reproduce the list in reverse order - 2 6 4 9 3, people have increasing problems with the task after the age of 45. This is confirmed in tasks where the subject has to remember the sequence in which lights are turned on and off. There are some work situations where such abilities are at a premium.

**Reaction Time.** The speed at which a person responds to a stimulus is made up of the time it takes the sense receptors to transduce the physical stimulus into nerve impulses (rods and cones take longer than hair cells) plus the time the nerve impulses take to travel to and from the brain to the muscles plus 'brain functioning time' or 'decision time'. It seems that as we get older our decision time increases. This is particularly evident in **choice reaction time** where any one of a number of stimuli may require any one of a number of responses.

**Social effects of ageing.**

In our culture, usefulness, acceptance, power, status and social contract have traditionally revolved around work. Cumming and Henry (1961) suggested that people feel rejected by society on retirement and continue a process of 'disengagement' from society. They point out that ageing is a continuing process but the artificial cut-off point of retirement creates fear and a sense of uselessness. According to disengagement theory, the retired person breaks off social contracts and withdraws from activities which would lead to interaction. This leads to increasing social isolation.

The social isolation of old people is increased in our culture by the effects of the breakup of the extended family (with grandparents living in the same house or nearby and fulfilling a role as childminders and houseworkers) and the move towards more nuclear families (husband-wife-children). With increasing mobility of workers (moving around the country for employment) old people are likely to be geographically distant from children and their families.

An old person's circle of friends will be gradually reduced as death claims an increasing number. However well prepared we are for the death of relatives and friends, the experience is stressful and draining, and the expression of grief is an important step in the return to normal life. It has been suggested by some that many old people experience retirement as a bereavement and go through a process of grieving for the 'lost' job and all that it signified in their past.

The whole process of disengagement and isolation is certainly exacerbated by our cultural attitude towards old age. As a group, old people are financially deprived, under-nourished, vunerable to physical attack and robbery, powerless, lonely, undervalued, and frequently forgotten. Many cultures value old people as workers or wise keepers of knowledge, but in our technological culture a person is valued by their ability to work and then more-or-less cast aside.

Improvement in the social conditions of the elderly will be the result of changing attitudes generally, rather than small scale schemes to 'care' for old people. Perhaps, as life-expectancy increases and more of us can look towards seven and eight decades of life, attitudes *will* change.

# 6

# CONDUCTING RESEARCH
# IN PSYCHOLOGY

## DATA COLLECTION AND INTERPRETATION

**What are results?**

When psychologists collect information, it is the result of counting events or people (eg. numbers of males and females, or number of eye-contacts) or measuring something (eg. the time a baby spends looking at a scrambled face). In fact counting is regarded by some as a form of measurement, but it has implications for how we treat the data when we analyse them.

The things that psychologists count are called **variables.** Both the independent variables (I.V.) and the dependent variable (D.V.) have to be counted or measured accurately as possible if our results are to be useful. (See I.V. and D.V. page 102).

It is not enough to measure and count accurately. We have to make sure that other people can understand our results. This means presenting them in a clear and concise form, often having to summarise them so that they can be taken in at a glance.

**Summarising and describing the results in pictures.**

1.   **Tables**

The most basic organisation of numerical information is a table. The data in a table are called *raw* data if they have not been summarised i.e. just a collection of measurements from subjects.

| | Table | | Number of eye contacts | |
|---|---|---|---|---|
| | **Independent Variable** | Subject | Condition A at 1 metre | Condition B at 3 metres |
| Subjects | **Dependent Variable** | 1 | 8 | 20 |
| | | 2 | 12 | 18 |
| | | 3 | 10 | 30 |
| | | 4 | 5 | 12 |
| | | 5 | 10 | 21 |

You can see at a glance from this table that results were collected from five subjects at both 1 and 3 metres (it was a repeated measures experiment) and that more eye contracts were made at 3 metres than at 1 metre in a two-minute interval.

## 2. Graphs and histograms

There are two types of graph, depending upon the type of data we have been collecting.

i) Counting can only be represented on a **frequency distribution.** Frequency distributions are very important graphical representations in statistics and psychology. If we measure the IQ's of a large number of people and count the number of people that have an IQ of 0, 1, 2, and so on right up the scale, we can plot a frequency distribution of IQ for the people we have measured:

Two ways of plotting frequency data:

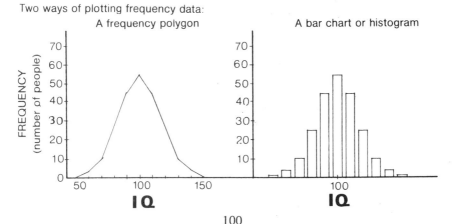

A frequency polygon

A bar chart or histogram

100

It is very important to label the axes of all graphs so that other people can understand your work.

The 'bell' shaped curve on our frequency distribution is characteristic of a **normal distribution.** Many traits, abilities and human physical measurements follow this shape and describe a normal distribution. This happens whenever the trait or ability is the result of many factors all acting at random to produce the measure. With all frequency distributions, the independent variable is on the horizontal axis and the dependent variable (what we have counted - the **frequency**) is on the vertical axis.

ii)  Measurements are represented graphically on **data curves** with the independent variable again on the horizontal axis and the dependent variable on the vertical axis. The graph below depicts the effect of different amounts of practice on the number of errors made in a mirror drawing task.

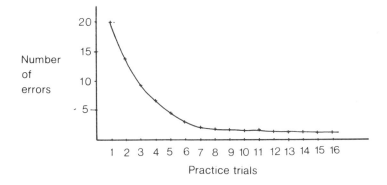

With a data curve you can see at a glance the effect that the independent variable has had on the dependent variable. In this case performance (as indicated by fewer and fewer errors) gets better with practice up to 10 trials, after which it has no effect.

**Summarising and describing the results in numbers**
**Descriptive statistics**
    If we have a large number of subjects and/or conditions it is sometimes not possible to see the effects of the I.V. on the D.V. at a glance. We then have to summarise our data numerically. This is not as difficult as it sounds - most people do it instictively when they say 'on average'.

101

The 'average' is a way of indicating where most of the scores lie on the scale of measurement. Eg. using the figures from our table onpage 100we can work out the average by adding up the scores and dividing this by the number of scores:-

$$\text{average (mean)} = \frac{\text{the sum of the scores}}{\text{the number of scores}} \quad \text{(this is called the \textbf{mean})}$$

so for condition A the mean $= \dfrac{8+12+10+5+10}{5} = \dfrac{45}{5} = 9$

and for condition B the mean $= \dfrac{20+18+30+12+21}{5} = \dfrac{101}{5} = 20.2$

It is now mush easier to see the difference between the two conditions.
It is also useful to know how spread out the scores are. A simple measure of 'spreadoutness' is the **range.**
The range is simply the difference between the top score and the bottom score:
    range  =  highest score - lowest score
so for condition A the range  =  12-5  =  7
and for condition B the range  =  30-12  =  18
We can now clearly see another difference between the two conditions - the results have different ranges.

**Drawing conclusions from data**
1.    **Experiments:**
    An experiment in psychology is just like an experiment in any other scientific subject; we try and keep all aspects of the situation constant except one, the **independent variable** (I.V.) and we change this in a very precise way. Take as an example the table on page 100 as the results of an experiment where subjects were made to stand 1 metre from an interviewer and the number of eye-contacts counted. Then the subjects were made to stand 3 metres from the interviewer and the number of eye contacts counted again. The independent variable (distance from the interviewer) is altered very precisely. If the I.V. is the only thing that has changed, then it must be responsible for any change in the **dependent variable** (the thing that we measure or count - in this case eye contacts). How can we be sure that nothing else is changing? We can never be 100% sure but we must make every effort to control the remaining irrelevant variables - the ways of doing this are listed on page 106. Also, of course it is foolish to think that the subjects mood, feelings and general state of mind will stay constant throughout the experiment - there are many things that could affect the results such as boredom etc. So the dependent variable is likely to change

for reasons other than a change in the I.V. - the D.V. may well differ due to **chance.** In order to ascertain whether this has happened, we have to use statistical tests (beyond the scope of 'O' level) and if we decide that chance *is* responsible for the change in the D.V. then we must accept the **null hypothesis.** (See page 105). If we conclude that the change in the D.V. really is due to the way we have changed the I.V. then we accept the **alternate hypothesis.** (See page 105).

2.    **Surveys:**

The purpose of a survey is to find out from a few people, the answers to some specific questions we are interested in and then make a guess that everyone else would answer in roughly the same way, if asked the same questions. This is a very risky guess to make. It all depends upon how similar the few people we choose are to everyone else. The few people are the **sample** and we have to make sure that the sample is representative of the population from which it is drawn (in this case 'everyone else'). There are three ways of selecting a sample, and the samples drawn stand a good chance of getting less and less representative as we do down the list:

**Random sampling** is when all members of the population stand on equal chance of being selected. This is *very* difficult, time consuming and costly to achieve. It can be made easier by **stratification** of the population, i.e. dividing the population up according to, say, age or occupation and selecting from each group.

**Systematic sampling** is when every, say, tenth name on a list such as the Electoral Register is chosen. There are many fairly obvious drawbacks to this.

**Quota sampling** this method involves giving each interviewer a quota of people containing a representative group of people of each age, sex, educational background etc. The problems with this is the selection of the quotas.

3.    **Correlation studies:**

A correlation is a statistical calculation telling us the degree of relationship between two naturally occurring events (see page 29). No variables are controlled or precisely changed as in an experiemnt, so we cannot say that one of the events measured *causes* another.

The calculation gives us a **correlation coefficient** and this can vary from + 1 (as one variable increases, the other variable increases) through 0 (no relationship between the variables) to − 1 (as one variable increases, the other variable decreases). Correlations can be graphically represented as **scattergrams** some examples are given below. However strong a correlation coefficient is, we can still never say that one variable causes the other. In fig.6.1 below, the type of teacher does not cause the exam results any more than the exam results cause the type of teacher. Either or both may be true, but a correlation study will not sort it out for us.

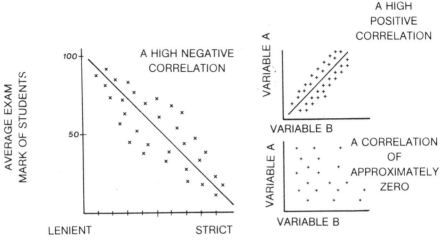

Fig. 6.1.

## FORMULATION OF RESEARCH QUESTIONS

The formulation of research questions in psychology generally, but not always, follows the methods of the natural sciences.

There is a series of stages evident when research questions are formulated and tested.

i)    The researcher recognizes or develops ideas about a problem in psychology which either appears not to have been tackled before or which the researcher feels would benefit from further research and clarification.

The researcher is making an effort to further understand and explain some type of behaviour and this forms the basis of her research question. The desire for further explanation may originate from a theory which the researcher feels uneasy or unsure about or from direct observation of some type of behaviour.

ii)   The observations or theories are examined and the problem is defined clearly. The relationship which it is thought may exist between the items under investigation is proposed in a tentative theory. This is known as the formulation of **hypotheses.**

In order to further understand the establishment of **hypotheses** a few scientific terms must be explained and then examples given.

104

Most research questions begin as hypotheses, ideas or propositions linking two or more **variables.**

In research the researcher is investigating the relationship between two things. These two things are called **variables.** For example, if the researcher is investigating the relationship between the amount of eye contact between two people and the distance at which they stand from each other, the two variables are eye contact and distance. The hypothesis which the researcher may propose concerning the relationship between these two variables could be that, as two people stand nearer to each other when having a conversation eye contact decreases, when they stand farther apart eye contact is increased.

The **hypothesis** therefore proposes a tentative idea about the relationship between the **two variables.**

Usually the experimenter establishes two types of hypotheses which she is aiming to test. These are —

1.   **The Experimental or Alternative Hypothesis.**

This proposes that there will be a difference between the two conditions of the experiment e.g. there will be a difference between the amount of eye contact made between people standing 4 ft apart and the amount of eye contact made between people standing 10 ft apart.

2.   **The Null Hypothesis.**

This proposes that there will be no difference between the two conditions of the experiment e.g. there will be no difference between the amount of eye contact made between people standing 4 ft apart and people standing 10 ft apart.

Thus according to the results the experimenter can accept or reject one or other of the hypotheses.

**The Alternative Hypothesis** can be phrased in one of two ways.

1.   **A one tailed alternative hypothesis.**

A one tailed hypothesis specifies the direction in which the results will go. e.g. There will be a difference in the amount of eye contact made when people stand 4 ft apart and 10 ft apart, more eye contact will be made when they stand 10 ft apart. Thus, this hypothesis is making a specific prediction, i.e. more eye contact at 10 feet.

2.   **A two tailed alternative hypothesis.**

A two tailed hypothesis just specifies that there will be a difference in the results, but does not specify the direction in which the results will go. e.g. There will be a difference in the amount of eye contact made when people stand 4 ft apart and 10 ft apart.

## Carrying out the Experiment

1.   The subjects should be selected by a process of random sampling in order to acquire a representative sample of the population. Random sampling should give every member of the population an equal chance of being selected e.g. pulling names out of a hat.

2.   In order that subject variables do not exert a **confounding influence** on the experiment, subjects are allocated to the experimental conditions in one of three ways.

   a)   **The Repeated measures Design.**
      Each subject takes part in both conditions of the experiment. If the repeated measures design is used conditions should be **randomized** or **counterbalanced** to avoid **order effects** occuring.
      Order Effects - If condition A is always presented first it may affect performance on condition B as the subject may be bored or tired.
      **Counterbalancing** - Where half the subjects do condition A first and then condition B and the other half do condition B first then condition A.
      **Randomization** - Where the conditions are presented to the subject in an order determined by chance.

   b)   **Matched-Subjects Design.**
      Subjects are matched into pairs (usually after having been given a pre-test), one of the pair takes part in condition A, the other one of the pair takes part in condition B.
      N.B. The subjects should be matched on variables which are of concern to the experiment and these may not necessarily just be age, sex and intelligence.

   c)   **Independent Subjects Design.**
      Half of the subjects are randomly allocated to one condition of the experiment and the other half to the other condition of the experiment.

When subjects have been allocated to the conditions each must carry out a **standardized procedure** indicated by **standardized instructions.** this is to attempt to avoid **experimenter effects.**
**Experimenter effects** - the effect that the presence of the experimenter can have on the subject's performance in the experiment.

Environmental variables, e.g. temperature, should not vary systematically across the two conditions of the experiment or the results will be said to be **confounded** (confused).

When the results have been recorded, they are considered using either descriptive statistics or inferential statistics.

Inferential statistics allow the calculation of the probability of the results having occured by chance factors and therefore give a basis on which to reject or accept our hypothesis.

# NOTES

# NOTES

729438

**NOTES**